Addicted to Perfect

A Journey Out of the Grips of Adderall

VITALE BUFORD

CHANGING LIVES PRESS

The publisher and author(s) of this book have used their best efforts in preparing this book. The information contained in this book is based upon the research and personal experiences of the author(s). The publisher and author(s) make no representation or warranties with respect to the accuracy, applicability, fitness, or completeness of the contents of this book. Therefore, if you wish to apply ideas contained in this book, you are taking full responsibility for your actions.

The publisher and author disclaim any warranties (express or implied), merchantability, or fitness for any particular purpose. The author and publisher shall in no event be held liable to any party for any direct, indirect, punitive, special, incidental or other consequential damages arising directly or indirectly from any use of this material, which is provided "as is," and without warranties. This book and its content are not intended as a substitute for consulting with your physician or healthcare provider. The publisher and author are not responsible for any adverse effects or consequences resulting from the use of material or information in this book.

Changing Lives Press
P.O. Box 140189 • Howard Beach, NY 11414
www.changinglivespress.com

Library of Congress Cataloging-in-Publication Data is available through the Library of Congress.

ISBN: 978-1-73225-848-8

Edited by: Michele Matrisciani
Cover design by Jade Buford
Interior layout by Gary A. Rosenberg • www.thebookcouple.com

Printed in the United States of America

10 9 8 7 6 5 4 3 2

Contents

This book is dedicated to Bentley Carter.
Thank you for showing me the way.

ONE

My First Time

"Here, try one of my Adderall," he says, like it's an aspirin. I've been dating Ryan for seven months now. He was diagnosed with ADHD when he was ten, so he has a prescription.

I'm taking eighteen credit hours this semester—which includes chemistry and a lab. Double majoring in public relations and fashion merchandising sounded like a great idea. Yeah right—who knew that chemistry was a requirement for fashion merchandising? And on top of my full course load I am working two part-time jobs—waiting tables at Cracker Barrel and clerking at a local boutique. I'm drowning. The stress of maintaining a social life with my boyfriend and sorority doesn't help, and I've gained ten pounds since the semester began.

I'm in my room in the sorority house getting ready for my shift at Cracker Barrel. It's embarrassing to walk out of my room in my brown apron, white button-down shirt, and black pants, so I change in the car instead. I don't want anyone to know that I work at Cracker Barrel because then they'll know how different I am from them. I'm already a year older, twenty pounds heavier, and not as put together. I don't need another reason to be different. On the way to my car, I pass by several of my sorority sisters—most of them are laughing and going to and from class. They seem so carefree while I am the opposite. All I do is care—what people think, how I look, what I say, what I do. They smile at me, but they don't engage with me. I feel like an outcast in the house I am supposed to live *in*.

I've heard of Adderall; people talk about it being helpful with studying. The only reason I know about this drug is because it was prescribed to my little sister, Frankie, in elementary school. She has ADHD and needed it to concentrate in school. It helped her stay focused and organized.

Adderall is a prescription stimulant that contains amphetamine, and it's used to treat ADHD and narcolepsy. Recreationally, it's used on campus as a study drug to pull all-nighters and to maintain the stamina to party. My sister was diagnosed with ADHD—she was doing poorly in school and was disorganized with little drive or motivation. Adderall helped her concentrate and focus, but she still struggled with school and was labeled a problem child. She still has that label. I make good grades—I'm a straight A student—but it's because I work my ass off. I am overwhelmed and I'm barely meeting the demands of college. It's the fall semester of my junior year—that means I have one year remaining to build the most amazing resume so I can get the most amazing job when I graduate.

When Ryan takes Adderall, it helps him study and stay focused but takes away his ability to connect with others emotionally. He becomes flat in response to conversation and, really, just can't engage. He's serious and short-tempered, and his eyes are lifeless. It's like Adderall cuts off his personality—he just focuses on schoolwork. Normally, Ryan is laid back and carefree, and Adderall steals that from him. Other side effects are restlessness and irritability and nervousness—it's why Ryan hates taking it. He just wants to smoke pot and chill, and Adderall is anything but chill. He's been watching me burn the candle at both ends—my anxiety makes my fuse short, and I'm not as fun as I used to be.

"Seriously—try one of my Adderall," Ryan urges. "It will help you stay focused and work faster; I promise." He hands me one of his Adderall pills. I hold it in my hand. It's 20 mg. It won't hurt to try it—right? Just this once.

Adderall is treated casually on campus. If you want it, you can get it. Easily. It's a miracle drug that gives you crazy energy to stay up all night and study. It's a performance-enhancing drug—the assignments that would typically take you several hours to complete take only thirty minutes on Adderall. It's like the controlled form of coke or speed or meth, but it's a prescription—so it must be legal. People with prescriptions sell it or give it away to people who crave it for performance. And now that I know about it, it seems like everyone is on it. I could walk into the student center or main library and probably find someone to sell it to me within five or ten minutes. How did I not think about taking this until now? I don't know if this is the answer, but I need something.

I go into his kitchen and turn on the faucet. I put the pill in my mouth, and I bend my head over the sink and turn my head to let the faucet water run into my mouth. I get enough water in my mouth and I stand up straight and I swallow the pill. I'm nervous—I have no clue how this is going to affect me. I go into the living room of my boyfriend's house and I sit down on the couch. He said it takes fifteen to twenty minutes to kick in. I'm looking at the clock, counting down.

I've stayed away from most drugs because addiction runs in my family. My mom would be sober one moment, and then the next moment she would walk back into the room completely drunk or high on Xanax. I learned to live by walking on eggshells. I also have a sister who is a drug addict who taught me to live on high alert—always in fight or flight mode—waiting for the tumult that would soon be brought on by one of her episodes and ultimately her run-ins with the law.

It was so lonely living with both of them. My dad traveled all the time for work so I was left with my alcoholic mom, who was always too busy running her business, and my sister, who was the imperfect trouble-maker. I wanted to be the opposite. And I was—I was the perfect child. I didn't make waves, I never argued, I always took a back seat to everyone else's attention mongering. I mediated arguments between my sister and my parents; in fact, I mediated arguments between my parents. I wanted everyone to get along. I did what I was supposed to do—make good grades, work hard, and look pretty while doing it.

I know the effects of taking Adderall when you don't have ADHD are similar to speed and coke—so, in the past, I didn't want to try it. I like to be in control. But I also like perfection. Maybe I will consider trading my control for the side effects—heart racing, sweating, intensity, stress, wired, sleepless, dry mouth, loss of appetite. I like drinking, but I reserve that for the weekends and the occasional weeknight. Building my resume, getting good grades, and working my part-time jobs are my priorities—making sure I get a good job when I graduate is my top priority. I need to stay focused and in control.

The tingling sensation in my fingertips begins on cue, just fifteen minutes later. My heartbeat speeds up. I feel hot sensations and suddenly have the need to be doing something—a shot of motivation. Beforehand, I didn't have the willpower to finish studying for my chemistry test but now that's all I want to do. I need to study and study and study. I grab my backpack. I head to the library and I study until 2:00 a.m. I've never studied that late—well, I have, but I've never studied that much. Usually I get distracted and take breaks, but not tonight. With Adderall I don't even stop to pee for six hours straight. There's something to this Adderall thing. It is a fucking miracle.

Ryan hates how it makes him feel, which is disconnected and lifeless. He doesn't care about his grades or achieving, he just wants to be present and enjoy life; Adderall takes that from him. He values living in the moment more than schoolwork. Which is too bad for him, but good for me, since he gives me half of his prescription. I take it to study and when I have days when I'm at work, and can use the extra energy, my Adderall is there for me. I love Adderall—absolutely love it. The best part? I'm never hungry when I'm taking it. I've been taking it for the past two months and I've lost twenty pounds—without diet or exercise. Adderall shuts off all the diet talk in my brain—and that's saying a lot because I'm always thinking about my weight and my body. I've lost twenty pounds. And I feel better than ever. I'm getting the best grades and I'm balancing my overloaded schedule—all with ease. I'm working two jobs and going to class full time, and I have a social life. Life doesn't get much better than this.

Everyone always talks up Adderall as the "study" drug. Fuck studying . . . I'm a size six! A few months ago, I was a size ten and at my wit's end. Now my fall semester ends with straight A's. It was my hardest course load yet, and I still manage to get the best grades since I've been in college.

It's Christmas break and time to plan for my spring semester abroad in Verona, Italy. I'll be there for three months. Ryan gives me some Adderall to use during the break—and I am grateful. This time it is strictly for weight control, since I don't want to gain weight before I leave for Italy. I won't have Adderall with me in Italy so I don't know how I'm going to maintain my weight loss, but I guess it doesn't really matter. I should be fine; everyone who has studied in Europe says you walk everywhere and lose weight.

The first month in Italy is one amazing party. I think there is only one day that I don't drink—seriously. The classes we take are a joke and don't take up much of my time, which leaves more time for partying, eating, and drinking.

Ryan and I are still together, but we find it difficult to maintain a long-distance relationship while living in different countries. I am the one having fun and experiencing new things, while he is doing the same old thing—going to class, smoking pot, going to work, and taking Adderall. God, I wish I had Adderall with me. If only I could eat all the pasta and pizza I want and not gain weight. But without Adderall I can hardly control my hunger—it's like I'm always eating. Always. I wake up and eat a traditional Italian breakfast that consists of bread and meat and jams. And then I eat lunch, which is either pizza or a sandwich. For dinner we always go to the Piazza to drink and eat more carbs. And then don't forget the gelato—it's amazing. It's no wonder I am gaining weight, but I don't know how to stop it or control it. If only I could somehow get access to Adderall here.

I daydream about it. I even devise a pretend plan to get it—my parents and sister are coming to visit me in a few weeks. Maybe there's a way my boyfriend could mail my sister some Adderall and then she could bring it to me. Or maybe my boyfriend could mail me Adderall—is that legal? I fantasize about Adderall—how to get it, how it makes me feel, how much weight I would lose if I had it. I wake up from all my fantasies and continue with my regular programming—eating, drinking, partying, traveling, and studying.

My parents and my sister visit me for a long weekend so we can visit my extended family in Naples. It is really neat meeting that side of the family, but it is overshadowed by my body shame. All I want is my mom's approval, but I can see the disapproval on her face. She is drinking a lot and I am drinking a lot, so we both ignore her disapproval. And all of my body shame is exacerbated by my envy of my sister's smaller frame. She's the perfect size six and I'm the oversized size ten. I am stuck with my mom and my sister and I can't run. I can't ignore my shame.

It is an incredible gluttonous three months, but I am ready to get back home. The only pair of jeans that fit me are a size ten and that is a tight squeeze. What will my boyfriend think of me? We haven't seen each other in more than three months. He probably won't be attracted to me and will break up with me. I mean—I would break up with me—I look disgusting. And then what will my parents think of me? And my mom? There's no hiding all the weight I've gained—I went from a size six to a size ten-twelve. I haven't weighed myself, but I'm guessing I've put on close to thirty pounds. I feel unlovable and ugly and fat. How could anyone love me like this? I'm playing out all the scenarios in my head. I have two weeks until I fly back to the states. Maybe I can stop eating and I will lose some weight? Maybe I can start dieting now—I will just remove carbs from my diet and stick with protein and veggies and salads. And definitely no gelato. No way. I feel so defeated—how did I let myself gain so much weight? Why can't I have self-control? No one else gained this much weight—I am the only one. Why couldn't I have eaten fewer carbs and drank less wine? Why do I always feel the need to indulge? I couldn't help myself—all the alcohol and all the food—I couldn't stay away from it. I mean—you only study abroad once so you should enjoy yourself. I did that. There's no hiding it and there's proof—my tight size ten jeans are proof. I'm surprised the seams haven't split.

I'm anxious as I board the plane to Atlanta. I'm physically uncomfortable from my weight gain. And I'm scared. Scared of what Ryan will think. There's no way he will want to kiss me or have sex with me—I'm too unattractive. It's been a long time since we've been together but he's expecting the size six version of me, not this version of me. I want this version of me to go away. I want the person I was before I studied abroad. She was happy. And I'm anything but happy. I can't believe I let myself go. Why couldn't I be one of those girls who lost ten pounds in Italy because she "walked everywhere"? Instead I'm the girl who gained thirty pounds.

I clear customs and head to get my luggage, and there he is, wearing the biggest smile on his face. How can he be smiling? I'm fat and ugly.

Maybe my weight gain isn't that noticeable? Who am I kidding—of course it's noticeable. We embrace and we kiss and all I can think about is the fat he's touching on the small of my back. There are extra rolls there now. I don't want him to see me—but you can't miss me—I'm thirty pounds heavier. I want to be invisible. I think about the fact that we are going to have sex at some point, and I dismiss the thought completely. I've never been comfortable and carefree when I'm naked, and I'm at my worst right now. I'm having thoughts about him leaving me because of my weight, the judgment on his face about my weight, the fact that I don't deserve love right now. How did it get this bad?

Ryan is the third person I've slept with—my first was my senior year in high school and the second person was a one-night stand in college. I was insecure then and I'm insecure now. I don't want to be seen, I want to be invisible. We get into the car and drive the four hours to Alabama. We are meeting my parents at my favorite Mexican restaurant—of course we are going to eat more food. I hope I won't run into anyone at the restaurant—I can't handle the embarrassment. Having my boyfriend see me is enough shame and embarrassment for today.

With the spring semester over, I'm stuck in Alabama while Ryan heads back to Atlanta for summer semester classes. My parents are breathing down my neck to find a job. I spent so much money in Italy, and they won't stop talking about it. I escaped this place when I left for college, and now I'm back here. And it's awkward. And my mom keeps telling me that I need to hang out with my sister and be best friends with her. I don't want to be best friends. I just want out. I feel trapped in my parent's house. I was supposed to take an internship in NYC at a fashion house and PR firm, but my parents said it would be too expensive to send me to New York. I need to find a job. So that's what I'm doing—what my parents tell me to do.

I'm a different person now. When I last lived here, I was in high school, I was thin, I had purpose. And I'm none of those things now. I apply for jobs because I want to make everyone happy—I want to be the perfect, obedient daughter. I was always praised for my beauty, but that's not the case right now. If I can't get points for how I look, then I might as well get points for getting a job. I feel that I need to do something to win back their affection.

I feel excommunicated since my return. I feel like a misfit, completely lost and out of place. I don't have any friends that are home this summer and I don't know how to relate to my family. Ryan is six hours away and we hardly talk. I have no friends, and I'm trying to figure out my family dynamic—I feel like I'm lost on an island and all alone. Plus, I don't want anyone to see me. I have so much shame about my body that I feel judgment from everyone—even the grocery store clerk. I can't get out of my head. I don't know how to integrate or if I even want to. I want to run, but I can't: I have to make my parents happy. I just spent a small fortune while traveling abroad and they are hanging it over my head. So I will find a job and work for the next three months until I return to school for my last semester of college. And that time can't come soon enough.

I feel out of place and fat and ugly in my house. My sister is thin, and I can feel my mom's disdain a mile away. I will be in the kitchen fixing myself something to eat and she'll walk in and I can feel her judgment. She has this look that she will give me—and she doesn't even need to say anything—she can cause a lifetime of pain nonverbally. She has a way of pursing her lips and there's the look in her eyes: it's pain projected as hate. I don't know what she's thinking so I make it up in my head—I tell my own story. And my story is dark. I'll be fixing something to eat and she'll say, "Are you sure you want to eat that?" I feel like a burden and that I'm taking up too much space.

My parents had visited me from time to time when I was at college. I was always stressed when they visited—my mom was unpredictable, and I needed to make sure my dad didn't get upset over my mom's drinking. And then my mom wanted me to include my sister with me everywhere I went while they visited. It created a lot of stress for me. One time during the visit, my mom could tell I was stressed—just being around her was a stressor. "I think you should try a Xanax, Vitale, to calm down," my mom said. "You are too stressed and it's too much. Here, take one." I didn't want to take it, but I took it anyway—she's my mom. Plus, I wanted her off my back. I took the Xanax and I was a complete weirdo—I just sat in the middle of the living room while everyone else was moving around. It was as if time had stopped. I couldn't get anything done. And for someone whose drug of choice is Adderall, Xanax has the complete opposite effect.

I hate applying for jobs—plus who the hell will want to hire me? I'm too fat. I don't want to leave the house because I'm afraid I will run into people who knew me in high school when I was thin. I can't take everyone's judgment. It's too much.

The one relationship in my life where I always feel loved and accepted is with my maternal grandmother. All my fond memories of childhood involve her, and she practically raised me. I remember her teaching me to cook and making her famous tuna salad with dill. She would take me to her hair appointments and to the grocery store on the military base where my grandad served in the army. She and my grandad were my caretakers when my parents were working—and my parents were always working. I feel safe with my grandmother; I feel loved. I want to see her and fill her in on my life and what's going on. I need to feel safe. I feel so unsafe at my house. Although my grandmother must know about my mom's alcoholism, I think she is in denial. She never speaks of it. Her way of dealing with it is to watch over my sister and me.

I go to my grandparent's house for lunch and to catch up with my grandmother—I can tell her everything—she's the only person in my family that I can trust. Maybe it's because she's sober—but I always know what to expect with my grandmother. She had polio when she was eleven and she's been disabled in some way ever since. Now she's in a wheelchair.

I don't see her as different; I see her as strong. And we are a lot alike— we are both left-handed, stubborn, bossy, resilient, control freaks, perfectionists. Since she is in a wheelchair and she isn't perfect, she never projects that onto me—the need to be perfect. I am perfect for her. I know what to expect with her, not like with my mom. I never know what to expect with my mom. One moment she's praising me for my accomplishments, and the next moment she's telling me I'm a terrible, selfish person for spending money in Italy. One moment she's telling me how pretty I am, and the next moment she's telling me she hates my boyfriend and giving me looks that clearly communicate her distaste for my weight gain. My grandmother is consistent. Her mood is always the same, the way she treats me is always the same. Even the day's schedule is always the same. I never have to question where I stand with her.

I walk into my grandparents' ranch style home and memories from my childhood flood into my mind. The good times I remember almost always happened here. My grandparents would pick me up from school every day and I would do my homework and eat a healthy snack—my grandmother was a dietician so she always made sure we ate balanced meals.

When I was a child, we had family traditions and celebrations around Thanksgiving and Christmas that were picture perfect. My mother is the middle daughter—her older sister Valary is divorced with no kids, and her younger sister Catheryn is married with two boys. I am really close to my cousins and spent summers at their house and went on road trips with them.

We had tradition and constancy and routine at my grandparent's house. During the week, I would sit down on the couch with my grandfather and eat popcorn with him while he had a Budweiser and I would watch the news with both of them until my mom or dad came to get me. We spent Christmas Day there and prepared our traditional meals together. My grandfather would take walks around the block with me and I would go out to their garden and pick fresh vegetables. It was a sweet childhood. I trust my grandmother with my life. She is a strong woman and she inspires me to be strong. She makes me realize that I can do and be anything I want to be.

When I arrive at my grandparent's home, I can hear everyone in the kitchen. I thought it would just be my grandparents, but I guess my mom and sister are here, too. This is the first time I've seen my grandparents since I got back from Italy—I've been avoiding my grandmother because I feel so bad about myself right now. She will know how unhappy I am, and I'm afraid of what she'll think when she sees me.

I walk into the kitchen and dining room area where my grandmother is in her wheelchair at her special place at the table. My mom is in the kitchen cutting up vegetables and preparing lunch. She turns around to see me and we lock eyes. I can tell she has something on her mind that she wants to tell me. I ask what we're having for lunch, and the disdain on her face is clear—I feel like I'm the target at the firing range. I'm fat and I'm asking about food.

"You are fat, Vitale," she says to me. This is the first time she's verbalized the look she's been giving me the past few weeks. I could feel it, but now I know it. Now there is no confusion about her feelings. It is as though she is waiting—like just her shame isn't enough—to shame me in front of everyone. She's made comments about my food choices before, but this is the first time she says it out loud and so directly. And she has an audience. No one says anything to challenge her so it must be true. I don't want to look anyone in the eyes because it's too much truth. Too much.

I've gained weight and I'm unlovable. I knew this would happen—I knew everyone would be disappointed in me. Her words echo in my ear: "You are fat, Vitale. You are fat." I'm equal parts angry and ashamed and broken. Isn't there a better way she could have handled this? Did she have to say it in front of my sister and my grandmother? I already feel terrible enough about it, and now I feel doubly terrible. I want to be invisible, but I'm far from that. I'm too visible. And now being too visible has its consequences. The consequence is that my own mother doesn't approve of me. My own mother thinks I'm fat and ugly. My own mother is embarrassed about me. I've let her down. And that's the last thing I want to do. I'm humiliated.

I spend the rest of my summer in complete self-destruction. I'm rebelling against my self-hate and I want to numb all of it. I don't want to feel my mom's hatred toward me. I don't want to deal with feeling fat and ugly and all that it entails. It's too much. It's too much feeling and emotion. I end up getting a server job at one of the local restaurants. I work from 10:00 a.m. to 10:00 p.m. and then I go out and party until 2:00 or 3:00 a.m. I want to drown my feelings with alcohol. Ryan and I break up over the phone and I feel lost. Of course we break up—I'm fat. I knew this would happen. I'm unlovable. My mom doesn't love me, my boyfriend doesn't love me—so I try to find love through sex and alcohol. I party and sleep with the head chef at the restaurant—so cliché.

I had begun using alcohol as a coping mechanism at the beginning of high school and then escalated when my first boyfriend, Jack, broke up with me. I tried beer for the first time when I was fourteen, and alcohol has been an escape for me ever since. I started drinking heavily on the weekends when I was in high school—it was an effective way to numb my teenage angst and offered me an escape from the volatility and neglect at home. But when my best friend from childhood, Matthew, was killed in a car accident, my whole world was lost. I couldn't understand how one of us could be dead. I didn't understand that I wouldn't really ever hear his laugh again or lay down next to him to tell him about my fights with Jack. Jack had been driving the car when Matthew was killed, and he and I divided further after our mutual loss of Matthew. I silently blamed Jack, and Jack had an unspoken blame and hate for himself. Ill equipped to deal with such big emotional questions and unresolved issues, we fell into this destructive habit of running into each other at parties and hooking up and then getting into enraged arguments. Always drinking. We'd be pulled toward each other the way people with shared histories are, only to hurt each other, as if we were punishing each other and ourselves for being alive when Matthew wasn't. This went on all throughout college.

My parents know how much I'm struggling—it's hard to miss. I sleep in until 10:00 a.m. and I don't get home until 3:00 a.m. Some nights I don't even make it home. I'm sure they're worried about me, but I don't care. My dad is always out of town for work during the week, so that leaves my mom and sister and me to our own devices. The contrast of normal, thin Vitale to this version of me is black and white. I am typically so put together and ambitious and disciplined. Not this summer. This summer I am a complete mess. My weight gain and life without Adderall have pushed me over the edge. All the way over. One night I let the head chef spend the night in my bedroom, and my dad comes to wake me up and finds us. That is the last straw. My partying and promiscuity are so out of control that my parents convince me to take the internship in NYC for the second half of the summer. I had wanted to do the internship all along, but my parents had said that it was too expensive. Plus, I am fat—how can I be fat and work at a major fashion house? Seems like an oxymoron to me. Fat and fashion don't go together. I had lined up the internship when I was in Italy—I had wanted to make sure my resume was graduation ready. And that means having a certain amount of internships and job experience. I am always good about that—thinking about the future and being strategic. And this internship and others are strategic—I want to get a big-time job in PR when I graduate. I want to have the perfect future. I've always been a go-getter and driven. I've always been so successful. That's why this summer is a complete anomaly—I am out of control.

Deep down I know my drinking and my behavior are destructive, so I agree to take the internship and spend the rest of the summer in New York City. I know that accepting it gets me out of my pattern of drinking and smoking and having sex with people I would never normally have sex with. Skinny Vitale would never conduct herself this way. But this is fat Vitale, and she doesn't believe she's worthy of much so she acts this way. I attract people and things that are unworthy of me because I feel unworthy.

I go to New York City, and it's just as I expect. It's a great experience, but I feel even more alone in the city. It's hard to make friends, and the size of my body is magnified by working in the fashion industry. Everyone I work with is rail thin and then there's me. They're all buying the sample sizes and leftover pieces that are size zero, and I can't fit one of my legs into one of those dresses. It's almost like I am asking to be punished for gaining weight. Oh, you want to feel even worse about yourself, Vitale? Okay then—let's move you to New York City for a summer and make you work in a fatphobic industry. Jesus. What am I thinking?

I sit outside my walkup apartment in Greenwich Village smoking a cigarette. It's a perfect location. I'm living with my friend's older sister while I'm here. I'm sleeping on her futon and my feet dangle off the end of the bed when I sleep, but it's worth it—I'm in New York City. I picked up smoking when I picked up Adderall, and the habit stayed with me. All the New Yorkers walking by are judging me for smoking, but I don't care. I already feel lonely and rejected so I'm numb to it. My phone rings and it's my mom. My grandmother has cancer and they don't know how long she has left to live. Fuck. This summer is the perfect storm—my world is completely falling apart. I've gained thirty pounds. Check. My mom called me fat. Check. My drinking is habitual. Check. My boyfriend and I broke up. Check. I'm fat and working in an industry that looks down on fat people. Check. And now my grandmother is dying from cancer. Check. My world has spun out of control.

I only know of one place to turn to solve all my problems: Adderall.

TWO

Passing the Test

My future depends on this doctor's appointment and getting a prescription for Adderall. I've decided it's the only way I can be successful. I need it to manage my senior-year course load, my internship, and my part-time job. Most important, though, I need it to lose weight. I'm sick of being fat.

If I can get this doctor to prescribe me Adderall, then I'm golden. No more problems, sadness, or being the overweight sorority girl. With Adderall, I will have it all together. I will be able to do it all. My heart is beating out of my chest as I think about the conversation I'm going to have with this doctor. My roommate Beth just got a prescription from him, but that doesn't mean I will get one, too.

Last night Beth and I were drinking Miller Lites on the back porch and she told me all the buzzwords I needed to say to secure my prescription. She reviewed the questions he asked her and all her answers. It was like I was studying for the hardest, most important exam of my life. If I don't get this Adderall, I don't know what I'm going to do.

As I stare into the mirror, I rehearse the lines, "Hi, I'm Vitale, and I'm having trouble concentrating. I'm so unorganized. And I'm having trouble staying focused." Beth told me the trick is to let the doctor think Adderall is his idea, not mine. I had the perfect excuse: I have a family history of ADD: my sister was diagnosed with it so it makes sense that I have it, too. I rehearse the lines over and over until it's go time.

"Hello, my name is Vitale Buford, and I'm here to see Dr. 1," I say to the receptionist. She directs me to take a seat in the waiting area. I don't think I actually sit down. I'm so tense it's almost like I'm levitating in the seat and I can't feel my body. I clasp my hands together with a tight grip. My jaw is clenched. I'm sweating.

I'm the only person in the waiting area when Dr. 1 comes out of his office. He mispronounces my name and he signals me to follow him into his office. My jaw is clenched so tight that, when I try to smile back, I can't. My name is always mispronounced—either that or people expect me to be a guy since it's a masculine name. I'm named after my dad's mom, Josephine Vitale Buford—it's her maiden name and it means "life" in Italian.

We sit down in his office and he asks the standard intake questions, "Tell me why you're here and what's going on with you."

I say my lines perfectly. "Yes, thanks for seeing me today. I'm having trouble concentrating with my schoolwork and I have a full course load, a job, and an internship. I'm having trouble getting things done and staying focused and organized."

He's actively listening and by the expression on his face, he's heard my story before. "Yes. I see a lot of these cases. Do you have any history of attention deficit disorder in your family?" Man, I can't wait to answer this one, especially since it's the only truthful thing I'll say during the entire appointment.

"Oh yes, my sister has ADD and so do my cousins, so it definitively runs in my family." I probably sound a little too excited in answering that question. But it feels good. It's like I am taking the most important exam of my life and I just slam-dunk the answer. He proceeds to tell me that he's going to prescribe Adderall for me and describes what the drug is used for and how I should take it. Of course, I already know this but act calm and interested. He writes the prescription and hands it to me—the piece of paper in my hand feels like the winning lottery ticket. He prescribes me regular Adderall, not extended release, and it's sixty 20 mg tablets for the month, with the instructions to take one or two per day based on my workload. I no longer need to get Adderall from Beth or some of her friends. It's all mine now. He says something about coming back in a month to see how I'm doing with the dosage. I'm trying to contain my excitement and appear natural, but I'm so fucking happy. This is going to be my cure-all. I have a high just holding the prescription in my hand.

I call Beth from the car. "I got a prescription!" She celebrates with me. I get off the phone and I feel content for the moment. I take a deep breath—all my nerves and anxiety are gone. I start the car and drive to the closest pharmacy.

* * *

It has been four months since my first prescription, and I don't know where the time has gone. I lost fifteen pounds in a matter of weeks, and I have been able to take on more shifts at work. I have the energy of ten people combined. I have always been successful with school and extracurriculars, but Adderall makes me successful times a hundred. Adderall takes me from good to great. Adderall makes me fucking perfect. And perfect is what I want. It allows me to take sixteen credit hours in school, plus work two internships, have a part-time job, and a social life. Adderall gives me the ability to be the most perfect student and intern while building the most perfect resume. And most important, it allows me to be thin. I can fit into size six jeans and store away my size tens. I don't have to worry about working out or Weight Watcher points. All I have to do is pop an Adderall or two and the pounds fall off me. I feel confident and safe and secure. Ryan is a distant thought because I don't need him—I have Adderall. I move a million miles an hour and my stress level is off the charts, but I look perfect on the outside, and that's all that matters. I feel stressed, overwhelmed, and busy but perfect as fuck.

I spend my days and nights jacked-up on Adderall. I get home from my daytime responsibilities and I meet my roommate Beth on the front porch to smoke cigarettes. Adderall increases my physiological stress level, making me feel restless and hyper, and smoking is one of the habits I picked up to counteract that. I don't even know if chain-smoking is an accurate way to describe the number of cigarettes I am smoking. I go from being a social smoker at bars to smoking a pack and a half a day. It is as if the Adderall revs me up so much that I have to smoke to keep somewhat sane. I need to smoke to decompress. I go through cigarettes like it is my job, and Beth and I smoke the hell out of them together. It is our nightly Adderall routine: come home, meet on our front porch steps and talk, smoke, and drink beer until one in the morning. Then we wake up at 7:00 a.m., pop our pills, and do it all over again. We are best friends and we are both addicted to Adderall.

I meet Beth at Longhorn Steakhouse for our weekly dinner. We sit down at the table and we order our usual: French fries covered in bacon and cheese for a shared appetizer, then salads with baked potatoes for us individually. It doesn't matter what we eat because we are on Adderall—we will only eat a few bites of the bad stuff anyway. I'm sitting across from her and she is blabbing away about her boyfriend who is away in Iraq and how much she misses him. I'm not really paying attention; I'm thinking too far in the future. *I need to finish that paper, complete that project for my internship, find a date to my sorority social,* I think to myself. I don't care what she has to say or update me on. I'm too consumed by my own thoughts or concerns. I order a Miller Lite because I just need something to take the edge off my Adderall high. I've taken twice the daily prescribed amount today and I'm on turbo charge. My tolerance for Adderall has increased in the past few months, and the usual 20 mg tablet isn't doing the job. I take it in the morning, but by the time the afternoon comes around, I need more. And although Dr. 1 told me to take one or two 20 mg tables, I need more like three or four to get me through the day. I've been getting so much accomplished and losing so much weight that I want more. I want more results; I want better results. I don't need to tell Beth this at dinner or ever because she knows what it does, too. We look at each other mid-sentence and we know it's time for a smoke break, so we get up to go outside.

I light my Parliament Light and she lights her Marlboro Light. I immediately feel a stress release. All my anxiety and stress and future-tripping melts further and further away with each puff. I look at her and she looks at me and we both know we have an Adderall problem. I then say it out loud, "We are chain-smoking, chain drinking, and chain Adderall-ing. It's gotten out of control. We need to do something about this."

"I know," she agrees. "Let's flush all of our Adderall in the toilet when we get home tonight; let's do it together. Let's make a promise to do this together."

"Yes, let's quit Adderall together," I say. I feel a rush of excitement. We can do this.

I walk into our apartment and run up the stairs into my bedroom. I keep my Adderall in a safe place in my jewelry box; that way no one can find it. I'm being a bit dramatic, but I don't want anyone to know about Adderall; that's why I keep it there. It's too important to me. It's the same jewelry box I got as a gift in middle school and my initials are on it. I used to keep friendship bracelets and love notes and mood rings in it; now it hides my secret stash of drugs. I open my jewelry box and remove the top tray, where beneath is my protected prescription bottle. I grab it and reluctantly open the lid. There are probably fifty pills left—about a ten-or-twelve-day supply, depending on how much I have to get done. *Do you really want to do this?* I think to myself. *Are you sure? Can you be successful without Adderall? What if you gain weight? What if you fail? What if you're not perfect?* I don't know if this is the right decision. I yell across the hallway to Beth, "Are you sure you want to do this?"

"Hell, yes," she exclaims. We meet in my bathroom with our bottles. Holy fuck, this is happening. I look at her and we both count down, "Five-four-three-two-one." I pour my Adderall into the toilet and she pours hers. We look at each other knowing it's the right thing to do, but we are scared shitless. Adderall is the solution to our problems. How will we handle our life now? How will we succeed? I flush the toilet and all the pills start swirling around in the water until they disappear. I immediately want my drugs back.

Beth and I never talk about Adderall again. It's as if the habit never happened. And we grow distant. She's working on getting accepted to nursing school and I'm in the middle of internships, schoolwork, and a part-time job. I'm glad we made the decision together, but I feel like it was the wrong decision, so I isolate from her, and I long for the drug. Coming off Adderall, I am tired, hungry, and cranky. And I'm pissed that I made that fucking commitment to her. If I had just saved some of the Adderall or not been so damn honest. Damn it. I adjust to life without Adderall. I mean I had been taking it for only four months, so I should be fine, right? I'm not that addicted. Normal life means working harder and keeping motivated and gaining weight and being unattractive. I hate normal life, but I adjust. I make do. I have only one-and-a-half more semesters until I graduate so I can do this. I can totally do this. The only thing that makes me feel better is smoking and drinking. So, I do that. I party and drink at night, and I go to class and work during the day. I am living life normally. And it sucks, but it's as it should be, I guess. Drinking numbs my feelings of being alone, fat, and ugly. Drinking numbs out my feelings of living a normal life. I hate living life normally, but I made a fucking pact with Beth so I've got to stick with it. And I that's what I do: I stick with it.

I gain back all the weight I lost on Adderall, which was about twenty pounds. I'm single, alone, sad, and fat. So I eat, drink, and smoke. It's a sad existence really. I long for companionship to feel whole. I long for someone to love me so I won't be lonely. If somebody loved me, then I would be worthy. My drinking leads to several one-night stands and self-hate. I fill the void in my soul with alcohol and meaningless sex. My naivety thinks one of these one-night stands will turn into a relationship, but I'm so wrong. It never does. I hate myself when I wake up in the morning, and I wait for the guy to be picked up by his friend so he can leave and never call me. I am worthless. I feel unworthy. If I were back on Adderall, all my problems would be solved. I would be thin and have a boyfriend and feel happy. Life would be so much easier.

* * *

I finish my last fall semester of college, and I head home for Christmas break. I go out drinking and partying, as all college kids do when they are home for the holidays. Except I hit it hard. I'm drinking hard liquor, taking shots, drinking beer, and blacking out. And then doing it all over again.

On one of the nights during my break, I'm out at the bar drinking and being loud and lively. I feel like the life of the party. Alcohol does that for me. It allows me to have fun. I take a shot of tequila, and I think I'm such a badass because I don't need the salt or the lime. I slam the shot glass down on the bar, and I grab my beer and turn around to sit down with a group of my friends. That's when I lock eyes with a boy I dated in high school, Greg. Except now he's playing football at the University of Kentucky, and he's much cuter than I remember. He broke up with me in high school because I wouldn't kiss him, which is funny to think about. I wouldn't have any trouble kissing him now. We say hello to each other and we talk all night. We laugh and catch up and I feel worthy. I feel attractive. Maybe he likes me? I end up leaving the bar with Greg and staying over at his friend's house. I'm drunk and I want him to like me and so I say yes to having sex with him. I will do anything for love and attention. The next morning, he drops me off at my parent's house, and I feel alone and hungover. I did it again. Another one-night stand. However, he calls me the next day, and we start talking on the phone, and this one-night stand turns into a relationship. We date long-distance the last semester of our senior year of college. He loves me and thinks I'm beautiful and ambitious, and I feel worthy. My longing for Adderall is gone because it has been replaced with Greg. He is my new drug. We are in love and talk about spending our lives together. I have found my person, and all is right in the world. I have everything I could ever need.

There's no way Greg would love the real me, so I play the part of the perfect girlfriend. I am a chameleon, and I become the person Greg wants me to be. He's a Christian, college-football-playing boy who wants to be in a relationship with a good Christian girl. So, I play that role. I am the perfect Christian girlfriend. I even go to church with him on Sundays. I don't want to lose him. And I don't know who I am anyway, so it doesn't hurt to try on this role for the time being. Who knows—maybe it is who I truly am. All I know is that he makes me feel worthy and I don't want to lose that feeling. Graduation day is approaching, and I begin looking for jobs in public relations and marketing when Greg asks me to move to Lexington. I feel so worthy: my boyfriend just asked me to move to the same city that he lives in. I must be doing something right.

With or without Adderall, I have a knockout resume and a strong work ethic. I search for PR and marketing jobs and I find an internship position available at a local PR firm. I apply. I interview with one of the account managers and she passes me along to the president, Pat. He interviews me and, instead of getting a paid internship, I get offered a job as his executive assistant. I accept the job and feel like my life is made.

As the executive assistant, I assist Pat with all his client work, which means I end up drafting news releases and opinion pieces and coordinating press conferences and client events. Oh . . . and running his errands. It's the job I've always dreamed of. I sit in on meetings with political figures and work on confidential projects. I've made it.

A few months pass, and the newness of my job and my new city dwindle. My old feelings of loneliness and unworthiness and imperfection are back. And they're haunting me. Greg is now a graduate assistant football coach. He's seldom around, and, when he is, he's preoccupied with football. I moved to Lexington not knowing anyone but him, and I'm fucking lonely. I don't smoke and drink like I used to so I start using food to cope with my loneliness and my boredom at work, and I gain ten more pounds. I'm already fifteen pounds heavier than I need to be so now I'm twenty-five pounds heavier. Every area of my life is sad and lonely. After about six months, I even become bored at the office. I wanted to be promoted by now, and I feel unworthy and unwanted. Lexington is not what I thought it would be. The dreams I have for living a perfect life are anything but perfect. I try working out to lose all the weight I've gained, but I don't have much success. I'm twenty-five pounds overweight, unhappy, and alone.

I begin daydreaming about the four months I was on Adderall. I was working on a million different projects and I was skinny and having fun. I sure as fuck wasn't lonely or imperfect on Adderall. I was whole and complete and perfect. I want to lose weight and I want to be motivated at work, and I start thinking about what it would take to get a prescription for Adderall again. It was so nerve-racking the first time; could I even do it again? Are the doctors in Lexington, Kentucky, like the ones in Athens, Georgia? Will the new doctor make me take an attention-span test to see if I am lying? I remember my sister having to take such a test when she was first being diagnosed. I will totally fail if this is the case. Some doctors are strict and require a test before diagnosis while others just ask for a list of your symptoms. I don't have ADD; I'm just hungry for perfection. I just need to be able to recite the right symptoms, which I have memorized. I have aced this part of the intake before with Dr. 1, and I can ace it again.

I remember the empty pill bottle in my jewelry box—I kept it even after Beth and I flushed all our pills. *Maybe I can get another prescription of Adderall with this empty bottle?* I had a habit of keeping my empty pill bottles—I had them stashed in random places in my car and in my closet. I kept them because I didn't want to throw them in the trash where someone could see them. I didn't want anyone to find out about my addiction. If I get caught, I could lose my Adderall, or, even worse, people would judge me.

The bottle is proof that I had a previous prescription, so it should be easy then to get another prescription? Who knows why I kept the bottle, but I did. I make an appointment with a family doctor under the guise of an annual physical. "I'm new to Lexington and I want to establish a relationship with a family doctor in case I get sick," I tell the nurse. Which is a fucking lie.

I arrive at Dr. 2's office and let him give me the annual physical because I don't want to appear drug-seeking. Before he finishes the physical, I find the perfect moment to ask him if he can refill my Adderall prescription. He looks at me a little confused, wondering why I'm asking him about it. I give him the sob story of me moving to Lexington all by myself for my first job and how I don't have a doctor yet. "Are you seeing any other doctors for your prescription?" he asks. I assure him I'm not. "I will only prescribe you Adderall if you see me exclusively," he continues. He explains that I cannot also go to a psychiatrist for a refill or get a prescription from another medical professional simultaneously, and, if that happens, he will terminate our relationship. Again—I could care less; I just want the piece of paper written for my Adderall prescription. I'll agree to anything and everything he says for that blue piece of paper. He grabs my empty prescription bottle and looks at the prescribed amount and then reads the label carefully, to make sure it's me. He quickly hands it back to me and pulls out his prescription pad and writes me the same amount I was originally prescribed—20 mg once or twice a day. He hands it to me and I grab it, but not too excitedly because I don't want to appear too eager.

I walk out of Dr. 2's office buzzing with hope. My life is about to be perfect once again. I feel so content with that piece of paper in my hand. I haven't even filled the prescription or taken the drugs; all I need is the idea of it. The possibility of it. Perfection is now within reach.

* * *

With my new prescription to Adderall, my life begins to change. Within two weeks, I lose ten pounds and take on new projects at work and start getting involved in my community. I am able to produce a high volume of work at the office and that makes me more valuable. My boss keeps giving me projects and I tackle them with ease. Pre-Adderall, I was able to draft one news release per day and now I am up to five. I am motivated and high performing, and I am getting praise for it. I am the perfect executive assistant and, within one month of my new Adderall prescription, I am promoted to account manager. Adderall is my gateway to success and opportunity. And the more I work, the more I feel valued. The more Adderall I take, the more I need.

Greg and I have grown apart. This isn't solely because we physically live in separate places; we are on different trajectories. When work is over, Greg wants to spend quality time together. Not me. Now that I have Adderall, I don't need him anymore. I am busy with work, and I like being busy. I don't have time for him anymore, nor do I want to spend time together. Our schedules are drastically different, and we value different things. He values football, hard work, and family. I value Adderall, success, perfection, and being thin. I don't need his love or attention anymore, and I don't care about returning it. I have been living in Lexington for about eight months, and my kind-of-good friends have turned into good friends, and my Adderall replaces my need for love and affection from Greg. Adderall makes me feel whole, worthy, and perfect. I am thin, successful at work, and have a group of friends I can count on. I no longer need him. My days are spent working on a million different projects, and my weeknights are spent working until one in the morning.

On the weekends, I party hard. Adderall gives me a high alcohol tolerance, so it takes me three drinks to get a buzz instead of one. Weekend nights are my chance to relax, party, and blow off steam. I go out with my girlfriends and pretend I am single and flirt with boys. Greg doesn't like going out and that suits me just fine because I am living life on my terms. I am all about me, all the time.

I get my third monthly refill of Adderall from Dr. 2, and this time I run out in two weeks. What should have lasted thirty to forty-five days only lasts me fifteen. My tolerance has increased, and I need more. When I first started taking Adderall, my prescribed amount would last me all day. In fact, I had leftover pills at the end of the month. But not anymore. Now I am taking what should normally last me two or three days in just one day. My normally prescribed amount starts to taper off around noon, and I need an extra push. So, I start taking more. And sometimes in the evenings if I haven't finished my work projects, I take an extra pill. I work until one or two in the morning because I can. My work and Adderall addiction become a habit. And the more I do it, the more my body adjusts to it—I require more Adderall to get through the day. My originally prescribed amount isn't cutting it. I do it because Adderall gives me energy, and I love the high of being busy and productive. It gives my life meaning—for once. Running out of Adderall is the worst possible thing that could happen because that means I have to be normal. Because of my increased Adderall tolerance, I run out of pills mid-month, which means only fifteen days with Adderall. Running out of Adderall feels like the world is ending. I can't refill my prescription until the next month. I hadn't run out of Adderall before. I am tired, depressed, angry, and hungry. I call in to work and tell them I am sick. I can't get off the couch because I am so depressed. I just want more Adderall. After two days of complete isolation, my friends, family, and Greg make their daily calls to me. I ignore all their calls.

Without Adderall, I don't want to live. I lie on my couch watching reruns of *Sex and the City* and bingeing on candy and pizza—anything to try to feel better. Except I feel worse. My body is craving calories because I hardly ever ate on Adderall and now it wants fuel. I am hungry and using food to cope with my feelings of loneliness and unworthiness. Once again, I am in a space of sadness, aloneness, and self-hate. I feel fat, ugly, and alone. My next prescription from Dr. 2 won't be ready for weeks. I know there is no way I can live on my couch isolated for fifteen days, so I start thinking of ways I can get more Adderall.

I could call Dr. 2 and tell him that I lost my prescription and that I need a new one, I think to myself. I call Dr. 2's office to do just that. I tell his nurse some big elaborate story about how I lost my prescription and that I really need another one. I hold my breath waiting for her answer, crossing my fingers that she would say, "No big deal, sweetheart," and ask Dr. 2 to write me another one. But she doesn't. "We are not allowed to write more than one prescription per month for this class of drug," she explains. I respond with a false smile and fake a goodbye that sounds like I am not desperate for Adderall.

I spend a third day on my couch and tell my boss that I still need time to recover from the flu—there's no way I can fake this for another ten days. I feel like I have the flu, but it is the Adderall flu. It's the kind of flu where you're weighed down in depression, self-hate, exhaustion, and hunger. I am covered in self-loathing, and it is all I can do to shower and put myself back on the couch. I do answer a few calls, so people don't think I am dead and come looking for me. That afternoon I finally realize I need to go into work the next day—I am afraid of the alternative and the possibility of losing my job. I get up to change *Sex and the City* DVDs, and I think about my first conversation with Dr. 2.

And then I remember Dr. 2 warning me about seeing another doctor for a prescription. And at this point I don't care—I don't want to live without Adderall. I need more and I need it now and I can't get another prescription from Dr. 2 until the next month. So I search on the internet for local psychiatrists. I call psychiatrist offices. The first four doctors aren't accepting new patients until the following year; I can hardly wait fifteen days, much less another six months. My fifth call is to Dr. 3's office. She has an appointment open for the following day, and I book it. Adderall will soon be mine again. I hang up the phone with a renewed sense of energy. My "flu" symptoms immediately disappear, and I get off the couch with a feeling of peace and comfort. Just the possibility of getting Adderall the next day gives me a high. I am ready to go back to being the perfect version of myself. I think about my appointment with Dr. 3, and I smile to myself.

I realize that I have to go through the whole dog-and-pony Adderall show for a chance at another prescription, but I don't care. I am becoming an expert in the game of Adderall.

It's day four post-Adderall and I get dressed for work. My clothes are tighter fitting than before my Adderall flu because I'm so swollen and bloated from all the bingeing I did over the past three days. I feel fat and ugly, but I know it will soon change. As soon as I get my next prescription for Adderall, I will lose the weight from the past three days and feel good again. Before I leave for work, I go into my childhood jewelry box and grab one of my empty Adderall bottles from Dr. 2. I head into the office to show my face and tell everyone exaggerations of my fake flu. I am unmotivated at work and exhausted, but I know it will change as soon as I see Dr. 3.

I search the internet for directions to Dr. 3's office and I write them down on an old receipt I found in my purse. I get in my car during my lunch break and follow the directions to her office turn-by-turn. I pull in the parking lot of a 1970s office building that houses many different medical offices. I walk in the front door and look for the sign to find the suite number and floor of her office. It is suite 210. I take the elevator to the second floor and find her office. I let the receptionist know I am there and I sit down. There are psychology magazines and old issues of *Reader's Digest* carefully laid out on each of the side tables. I wait patiently for my name to be called. I look at my watch and she is running thirty minutes behind. I think about everyone at work; they are probably wondering where I am once again, but I don't care. I need my Adderall and I will wait all day if I have to. Her prior appointment exits her office and I wait for her to call my name. "I'm ready, Dr. 3. I need my Adderall," I think. I play out our conversation in my mind: what she will ask me, what I will say. I envision her writing me a prescription, and it makes me feel so fucking happy. Dr. 3 finally comes out into the small waiting area and calls my name, "Vitale, I'm ready for you."

Dr. 3 must be seventy years old. She's wearing wire-framed glasses and her hair is short and colored a dull brown—it makes me think of the times I would go with my grandmother to get her hair colored at her hair salon. I follow her as she walks back to her office ever so carefully and slowly with her cane. I find a seat across from hers and sit down slowly and cautious- ly—*I hope this works out.* "So, tell me why you're here today," she asks. I give her an edited version of me and tell her the sob story about my recent move to Lexington and how I don't know anyone. "My job is demanding, and I have so much trouble concentrating," I begin. It's a fucking lie, but I go with it. I'm becoming an expert at manipulating doctors for Adderall. "I've been seeing a family doctor for my Adderall prescription, but I think it's time for me to see a psychiatrist, someone like you," I explain. I want to build up her ego and make her feel needed—it's part of my game. She agrees of course— because she's a psychiatrist and she wants my business. She asks me the standard ADD questions and I answer them perfectly. She then asks for my old prescription and I reach into my purse and hand her the empty bottle of Adderall from Dr. 2. "Ten milligrams twice daily," she says out loud to herself while she's processing what dosage to prescribe me. "I'm going to prescribe you twenty milligrams extended release twice daily. This will give you a continued stream of the medicine, so you can be effective all day long." Extended release Adderall or Adderall XR is different than regular Adderall. I've never tried it. She says that it's stronger than regular Adderall because of the extended release formula. I don't care what she's prescribing me; I just care that it's Adderall. I feel like I'm winning today—this new Adderall is like a promotion. I nod my head and act interested in what she has to say. She pulls out her prescription pad, and she writes me three prescriptions with dates for this month and the following two months. I never had predated prescriptions. "I've hit the fucking jackpot with Dr. 3," I think. Before she hands me all three prescriptions, she pauses. "You will need to stop seeing your family doctor from now on," she says. "I will take care of you from here." I shake my head yes—I will agree to anything at this point. I schedule my next appointment with her for three months from today and I head back to my car. Holy fuck, I did it.

I fill my new prescription, and this dosage of Adderall makes me feel on top of the world. The 10–20 mg dosage of regular Adderall is nothing compared to 20 mg XR twice a day. I'm on fucking fire at work. And the pounds fall off me even more. I've lost fifteen pounds in four weeks and

I feel so whole and worthy. I feel safe with my Adderall—I don't have to worry about my weight or being imperfect. And I have two more prescriptions, so I'm not concerned about running out. I'm taking my new dosage as prescribed because it's XR and my body isn't used to it yet. I'm used to lower doses of regular Adderall and XR is much more powerful—plus, I'm taking 40 mg of it. This is the real shit. Adderall gives me physiological anxiety and stress, so I smoke to calm myself during the day and binge drink on the weekends. Greg thinks everything is fine with us, but it isn't. I'm bored with him. I want to go out and party, laugh, and live a big life. I don't want to be a football coach's wife. I want to have my own big important career. I have other men lined up just in case my current relationship ends. That's what I'm like on Adderall—all about me.

We both drive home to Alabama for the Fourth of July holiday, but we drive in separate cars. My friend Morgan comes home with me, and I think she will have fun partying with me and some of my high school friends. Greg hangs out with his friends and I hang out with mine. He can tell I'm pulling away from him. We talk on the phone, but we don't even see each other even though we're both visiting our hometown. He thinks we are going to get married soon, and my mind is focused on the next best thing.

Morgan and I go out partying and I'm jacked up on Adderall and beer. It takes a lot to get me drunk because of how fast I metabolize alcohol with my new Adderall prescription. We are out at the bars partying like it's a high school reunion and I run into Jack, of course. I know in many ways I am over Jack and he is over me, but what we are both not over is Matthew and our history growing up together and experiencing rites of passage like first dates and first kisses. Damn, I think. I want to catch his eye. He was my first kiss at age sixteen. And, like our pattern always dictates, we end up drinking and partying together all night just like in high school and we tell each other how much we like each other, although it means nothing because we are both basically beyond any common sense. I'm surprised I even remember the conversation. We all end up spending the night at a mutual friend's house, and Jack invites Morgan and me to a lake house party the next day. I gladly accept, with no concern for Greg.

We head out to the party and I'm filled with excitement and remorse. Excitement that I get to see Jack, and remorse for lying to Greg about my whereabouts. I know it's a bad idea and feel guilty and unsettled for lying to Greg, but I want what I want. After an hour-long commute, we arrive at Jack's lake house and it's all my closest high school guy friends. Everyone has already started drinking and we join in. Morgan sits on the sidelines nursing her hangover, and I turn all my attention on Jack. Both of us proceed to drink way beyond our limits and I wake up the next morning beside him completely naked. We must have had sex. *Fuck, I cheated on Greg*, I think to myself, completely hungover. No good decisions come out of Adderall and alcohol.

I am overcome with guilt and regret on the drive back to Kentucky and I can hardly think a positive thought. Morgan knows I cheated on Greg so there's no hiding it. I have to do something about it now. I end up breaking up with Greg for the chance to be with Jack, but it turns out Jack doesn't want me either. I'm left alone and feeling worthless once again. I have my Adderall, but it's not enough. I need to feel wanted and desired by a man. I need to be perfect. I think obsessively about what I did to Greg, and the fact that Jack doesn't want me. I lament; it all keeps me awake. I've always been a worrier, but since taking Adderall, I notice I have become obsessive. Another by-product of Adderall is that it aids obsessive thinking. My brain is like one hundred open tabs on the internet. I have so many task lists going on 24/7. I can't stop thinking about my work projects and the errands I need to run, and the birthday present I need to buy for my friend's birthday party. I can't stop thinking about my broken heart. Not just Jack. But Matthew—why am I alive and he isn't? I allow myself to cry; I pop another Adderall. I have too much work to do to be crying.

My personal life is going to hell, but my professional life is going exceedingly well. I get assigned several new clients and one of the projects is public affairs work for a local referendum, and I'm working seven days a week and loving it. My Adderall tolerance continues to increase, and my third prescription from Dr. 3 is ready to be filled. I also received another prescription from Dr. 2 in the mail because I didn't stop seeing him when I started seeing Dr. 3. I continue to see both doctors because I don't want to run out again. I think about what it felt like to have the Adderall flu, and I never want to feel that way again if I can avoid it. I figure there's no way Dr. 2 and Dr. 3 can find out about each other anyway, so I head to the pharmacy to fill both prescriptions. I naively hand the pharmacist both prescriptions to fill. She grabs both pieces of paper, and, as she's reading both prescriptions, she notices that they are written by different doctors. She seems confused, so she double checks the information written on the prescriptions. She looks up at me and pauses. "You can't fill prescriptions from different doctors for these types of drugs," she says sternly. The look of condemnation on her face sends shocks of anxiety and shame throughout my body. I am overcome with guilt and fear. *Am I in trouble? What does this mean?*

She accuses me of "doctor shopping," which I know nothing about. She keeps both prescriptions and tells me that she is going to call both doctors and let them know that I tried to fill both of their prescriptions. I go from feeling on top of the world to feeling like a criminal in a matter of seconds. I didn't realize you couldn't do that, or that doctor shopping was even a thing. I am a naïve Adderall junkie—I'm still learning the role. I feel like all eyes are on me and I'm in the spotlight, and not for a good reason. It reminds me of when my mom called me fat—it's a completely different situation, but the shame is the same. I feel shame for my addiction and for not knowing better. Of course, I can't fill two prescriptions from different doctors—why couldn't I have just been more thoughtful? Instead, I was greedy. I wanted all of the Adderall. Not only am I going to lose access to my Adderall, but I'm going to get in trouble with my doctors. A thousand different scenarios play out in my mind—one scenario, I get a call from the doctors and they yell at me; another scenario, I'm getting arrested by the cops for doctor shopping; and another scenario, I'm fifty pounds overweight and I can't stop bingeing.

I don't know what to say or do and I don't want to cause a scene at the pharmacy. I don't want the other people in line to overhear what is going on. I was already being judged and shamed by the bitchy pharmacist. I don't need judgment from anyone else. My heart is racing. I step out of the line; my eyes are focused on the floor—I don't want to look anyone in the eyes right now—it's too much shame and judgment. I walk out of the pharmacy empty-handed and scared shitless. I don't know what my consequences will be. I go home and smoke three or four cigarettes before fixing myself dinner. I feel like a failure and a criminal. *How did this happen to me?* At least I have a few 20 mg XRs left for the next few days.

I wake up the next morning and my muscles are tense from all the anxiety of the events from the day before. I don't feel like living or going on—how am I going to get Adderall? After a few hours at the office, I get a call from Dr. 3. "Vitale, we received a call from the Kroger pharmacy yesterday," she says. "I need you to come in this afternoon and see me." My heart sinks into my stomach. I have no idea what my consequences will be. This could be the end of my Adderall career. This could be it.

I walk down the hallway toward Dr. 3's office, and my feet feel heavy, like I'm walking on sand. I open the door to her office and notify the receptionist of my arrival. I sit in the waiting area for forty-five minutes until she comes out to see me. "Hi, Vitale," she says. "I'm ready for you." I follow her slowly to her office and sit down. Every muscle in my body is tight. It takes her awhile to get situated in her chair—her age is showing. "We need to discuss the call I received from your pharmacist," she says. "Okay," I respond. My heart is beating faster and faster. "When we met last time, I thought I told you that you couldn't see your family doctor anymore," she begins. I have a few seconds to come up with my response. What should I say? "I'm not sure I understood when you told me that," I explain. "Anyway, it was my last prescription from him. I'm really sorry, Dr. Three. It won't ever happen again." A thousand different thoughts are swirling around in my brain. I'm holding my breath waiting for her to respond. I don't know if it was the sad look in my eyes or my tone of voice or her old age, but she bought my lie. "Okay, well. There must have been some confusion," she says. "Just make sure you don't do that again or I won't be able to work with you." She sends me off.

My Adderall supply isn't cut off, but my tolerance is getting higher and I need more Adderall to make it through the day. I no longer have multiple prescriptions from two doctors. I only have my post-dated prescriptions from Dr. 3. I need to figure out a way get more Adderall in between prescriptions. One prescription isn't lasting as long as it used to, and I can't go a few days without it again. I think of some of my friends who have prescriptions that might be willing to sell or give me a few extra pills. The only people I can think of are my married friends from college, Rebecca and John. The three of us studied abroad together in Italy and became really close. They both have Adderall prescriptions—they always talked about taking it for exams and studying. I'm sure they would sell some to me. They both have ADD and actually need Adderall; they don't abuse it like me. But they know people abuse it and I'm sure they would be open to me buying it from them. Anything for some extra cash. The only problem is that they live in Knoxville, which is 180 miles away. I don't want to run out of Adderall again, and I start calculating the drive time. *I've driven there for a weekend before; I could definitely drive there roundtrip in one night.* I brainstorm about how I can ask them for Adderall, and then I realize I would come off as an addict if I tell them I am driving there just to buy Adderall from them. Plus, I don't want them to think I am using them for Adderall, even though I am.

I devise an elaborate lie about being in Knoxville for a marketing conference, and I ask if I can meet them for dinner when I'm in town. Of course, they say yes because we are college besties and traveled abroad together and I was a bridesmaid in their wedding. We called ourselves the three amigos before they got married. They had a lot of Adderall between the two of them, or so I thought.

I leave work early the next day and drive 180 miles to Knoxville—I'm speeding and smoking cigarettes and listening to Fleetwood Mac on repeat. I'm on a mission for Adderall. I know what I am doing is crazy, but I don't care. Adderall is my God and I need to be perfect. I meet them for dinner, and I lie to them about the fake conference I'm in town attending. I had even researched hotels in case they asked me where I was staying, which is nowhere since I am going to turn right back around and make the drive home. We are in the middle of dinner when I finally find the perfect opportunity to mention Adderall. They knew I was taking Adderall my senior year of college, and I knew they took it, so it is no secret between the three of us. "Any chance either of you have Adderall I can buy?" I ask.

"I have some big work projects coming up and it would really be useful." I hold my breath waiting for their answer. I want to make sure it doesn't sound like the reason I asked them to dinner, but I also need to know if they have it because I have another 180 miles to drive back to Lexington after this. "I don't have much left, but I can sell you a few," says John. Ugh—my heart sinks. I just drove two-and-a-half hours for a "few pills." I'm only twelve months into my Adderall career but I'm hooked and I'm playing for keeps. I rush dinner and tell them I need to get to bed soon since my "conference" starts bright and early in the morning. Jesus. I'm lying and manipulating and it's starting to become second nature to me. I meet them at their house for the Adderall exchange. John says he can sell me fifteen 20 mg Adderall pills. It's not a lot but I will take what I can get. I hand him $50 and I tell them I'm headed to my fake hotel for my fake conference.

Who am I? How have I turned into someone who drives five fucking hours for fifteen Adderall? Who lies to her best friends who trust her? Who has the audacity to try to pick up two prescriptions at once? I don't know who I am, I just know that I long for validation, perfection, and professional success. I start my car, light a cigarette, and take the exit for 75 South to Lexington.

THREE

Adderall Extremes

It has been two years since graduation, but Beth and I still keep in touch. In fact, her wedding is getting close. Ever since the night we flushed our Adderall together there has been a distance between us, but she is marrying her college sweetheart and I am excited to be on Amelia Island for her mid-July wedding.

My parents were invited, so it is a family affair. I am flying down and they are driving and picking me up at the airport. The three of us are sharing a room together—that will be interesting. The last time I was home, my parents were arguing a lot and my mom was up to her usual drinking and my sister was causing the usual drama. It was complete chaos. I'm not sure why I thought it would be a good idea for all of us to go to the wedding together—but I didn't think it through. Maybe being on the beach is exactly what we need—maybe it will help our relationship. Honestly, I am just glad they are paying for everything since I am not making enough money to afford the trip on my account manager's salary. It is an interesting dynamic—I want to be away from the chaos, yet I can't get away from the chaos. It's comfortable to me. I can't wait to be reunited with my friends from college. I am back on Adderall full time, and that means I am thirty pounds lighter than the last time they saw me. I can't wait to show off the skinnier, better, prettier version of me. My new clothes and new confidence and new body.

My parents pick me up from the airport and I am jacked up on Adderall. I had taken my usual four 20 mg pills in the morning, and I will take a few more later. My mom is sober—thank God. That's one less thing to worry about for now. My parents go on and on about Frankie's most recent drama and I am trying to tune it out. They are excited to be out of town, but they are also nervous—who knows what kind of trouble Frankie will get into while my parents are out of town. She just turned twenty years old, and she dropped out of junior college and is still living with my parents. It's a constant stream of drama. Which is one of the reasons I hate going home. I am sick of Frankie always sucking the energy out of the room, even when she isn't there.

We arrive the Thursday before the wedding and there is a welcome party for the people who are there early—it is an excuse for all of us to get really drunk together. I get dressed up and leave my parents to their own devices, and I head to the party. There is this one guy, Jason, that I had a crush on in college. He is one of the groomsmen and I had hung out with him a few times when Beth and George were dating. I am excited to see him—especially with my new confidence and my new body. I feel on fire. I walk into the party and by the looks on people's faces, I am hardly recognizable. They are used to overweight, college Vitale—not the thin, successful, confident Vitale. I feel so good and so confident—and I owe it all to Adderall. The entire weekend ends up being a drunken shitshow. I end up coming back to my parent's hotel room at 4:00 a.m. one night because I hook up with Jason. I am lonely and I am afraid and I just want to feel wanted. And so I drink excessively and take Adderall and party and look for affection.

On the last day, my parents sit me down. "Vitale, we need to talk to you about something," my dad says. I figure this has to do with my ridiculous drunken behavior from the weekend. I roll my eyes, I feel defensive. I have already judged myself for my slutty behavior, I don't need my parent's judgment, too. I sit down on the couch across from parents, who are sitting on the edge of the bed next to each other. I am hung over from the night before.

"Vitale, we need to talk with you," my dad repeats. "Okay," I reply. There is a long pause, and then my mom interjects, "Vitale, your dad has cancer." What? I have no words. I am speechless. I thought they were going to lecture me on my drinking, and instead they are telling me about my dad's diagnosis. Is it fatal? What kind of cancer? How long have they known? What are they doing next? I have so many questions and yet no words.

My dad has always been my protector and my confidant and my role model. My freshmen year of college was terrible—I wanted to quit school and transfer to Auburn—in fact, I had already completed the paperwork. I was so lonely at Georgia, so alone. My dad was working in Atlanta during the week and he made sure to have dinner with me twice a week for six months. He saved me. He saved me from a deep depression—he saved me from loneliness. My dad taught me how to dry my hair when I was seven, and he makes the best homemade macaroni and cheese I've ever had. Whenever I need professional advice—he's the one I call because I admire how he became successful from nothing. He never went to college, and he started doing shift work at a paper manufacturer and now he is in charge of an entire region for the same company. Plus, my mom is the alcoholic and my dad isn't—it's that simple. I am always comparing them. Anyone looks good next to my mom. And now it is my "good" parent that is sick. It is my "good" parent that might die.

My parents drop me off at the airport and tears start pouring down my cheeks as they drive away. They don't know the prognosis of my dad's throat cancer, but they promise to keep me informed. I feel so alone. I walk into the airport and the first thing I do is find some water so I can take my Adderall. I need to focus on something else, anything else. So I get into work mode—which is my escape from reality.

Work and weekend partying—both of my escapes. They fuel each other. Being jacked up on Adderall during the week makes me want to blow off steam on the weekends. And then my behavior on the weekends (the parts I can remember) make me want to escape into work. The two must coexist. And I can't exist without my Adderall. I need the Adderall to be thin and perform at work and be perfect. And I need the Adderall on the weekends so I can be thin and confident and drink. It is a toxic combination—but it works for me. Plus, I thrive in the chaos and the drama. The more chaotic my life is, the safer I feel. I thrive off extremes. I am either working until 2:00 a.m., or I am drinking and partying until 3:00 a.m. It is just like my mom—she owns a successful travel agency—and she is either buried in her business or she is buried in a bottle. I never know which version of my mom I will be getting at any given moment. She can walk out of the room sober, and walk back into the room drunk. I remember the first time my parents met Beth. We went out to dinner in Atlanta and alcohol was being served. My mom went from the sweet woman I know she can be to the controlling bitch she always becomes with alcohol. "You don't need to be eating that, Vitale. Are you sure that boy likes you? You need to work harder," she would tell me in front of Beth. I am never prepared for her alter ego, yet it is always constant.

Sometimes chaos looks like working seven days a week and partying two to three nights a week. Sometimes chaos looks like hooking up with random guys on the weekends, and sometimes chaos looks like getting in the middle of the family drama between my sister and parents. No matter which way—chaos is my calm. I even yearn for the chaos of Adderall. The chaos and drama feed me when I am trying to get a new prescription or lying about misplacing a prescription just so I can get more drugs. I crave the drama.

I am up to 120 mg XR daily—I take three 20 mg XR in the morning and then 20 mg XR in the afternoon. If I have a lot of work to do, I take a few extra in the evening to keep me going. I stay up until 2:00 or 3:00 a.m. working and am only getting two to three hours of sleep each night. The only way I can physically function is with Adderall. I need it to stay up all night, and I need it to stay awake during the day. It is my own chaotic world that I have created. And I love it. I thrive off it.

I can eat anything I want—cookies for breakfast, Mexican food for lunch, and pizza for dinner—basically all my favorite food groups. I can eat whatever I want and not gain weight. In fact, the more Adderall I take the more weight I lose. Even when I eat unhealthy food, I don't eat much of it because Adderall decreases my appetite. I take a few bites of pizza and am done. When I am starving and eat a lot, it doesn't matter. With Adderall, I have the metabolism of a seventeen-year-old boy. Adderall is the key to being thin. Which means it is the key to being perfect. If I am skinny, I am happy. If I am skinny, I am worthy. If I am skinny, I am perfect. If I am skinny, people will love me and accept me. If I am skinny, I am successful.

Besides being ultra-thin, I smoke like a chimney. I smoke in the morning and on the way to work and during my lunch break and on the way back to work and before dinner and after dinner and all throughout the night. In fact—it must be more than a pack a day. You get the gist—I am smoking a lot. A whole lot.

Other "perks" of Adderall include dry mouth and sweating. My mouth is dry yet I am always sweating—it is a paradox. I ruin many blouses because of my excessive sweating. My metabolism is on hyper mode and that means I sweat so much there are certain fabrics and colors of clothing I totally avoid wearing because I am afraid people will be able to see the sweat stains. Seriously—besides being on overdrive, I am constantly worried about sweating through a shirt or dress or ruining clothing. And I ruin a lot of it. My lips are dry because I am extremely dehydrated. I am always in "go" mode—in the Adderall zone—which means I am intense and hyper focused. I don't have time to eat or drink, and I don't even stop to think about it.

Intensity is another side effect. I am intense—all the time. I mean— all the fucking time. My intensity is related to the fact that I operate in extremes. I'm either all on or all off. One person might work a 9 to 5 job, but I work a 7 to 8 job, with no lunch break. My idea of half-assing something is doing it over or revising five times instead of six. One time, I worked on a project until 5:00 a.m. to make sure it was finished, and then I went to sleep and got up two hours later to go back into work. And this is normal behavior for me. Lots of work and little sleep. There isn't one thing I am not extreme about. Whether it be about work or drinking or boys or friends or family—I am intense. Which means I don't go out on the weekends unless I am closing the bars down, I don't open a bottle of wine without planning to finish it, I don't make a friend without shooting to be in her wedding party, I don't join an organization without planning to become the chairperson. A friend once suggested that we leave a half-bottle of wine unfinished at dinner, and my answer was to finish it.

Then there is the tardiness. I am always late. To everything. I even set all my clocks ahead, and I will still be late because I am concerned only about me. I am on Vitale time. I will start getting ready to meet my girl-friends for dinner or for a work appointment, and I will get distracted by something else. And because I am hyper focused, I will do that other thing intensely until I realize how late I am going to be. I am always driving like a maniac on two wheels, smoking a cigarette, trying to get somewhere late. I am constantly in a hurry. In fact, I live in a hurry. Rush should be my middle name. It is all about me. And when I do finally arrive to said destination, I am not present because I am always in the next moment or project, not the moment or experience or person or project in front of me. My mind is constantly racing and constantly going and going and going. I am always going.

My health suffers because of poor nutrition and stress. Adderall quiets my hunger. I am never hungry, and when I do eat, it is pizza and cookies or Mexican food. I am not getting the proper nutrients—pizza and cookies will only get you so far. Plus—I am stressed all the time. I get sick fairly regularly, but I power through because being productive is the only thing I know will make me feel better. Rest is not my thing. My hair is thin, and my nails are brittle because my nutrition is poor.

There may be negative side effects, but the positive side effects outweigh all of them. I don't care if I am sweating and smoking and intense and running late. What matters is that I am perfect. What matters is that I am high-performing and successful. What matters is getting praise for my achievements. What matters is being thin. What matters is being able to party hard on the weekends. What matters is perfection.

My dad's cancer is diagnosed as stage 3 cancer, but the doctors say the odds are in his favor. If they can surgically remove the cancer and then do chemo treatments, his survival rate is high. I am removed from most of the experience because I live six hours away by car. I am really removed from it because I choose to be. To face my dad's mortality is too much for me. I am a daddy's girl. My mom is the alcoholic and my dad is not the alcoholic, so that means I love him more. Or maybe it means that he hurts me less. And all I want is to hurt less, so I numb the pain of my dad's cancer. I numb the pain of potentially being parentless. Being without a dad. I bury it and pretend it isn't happening.

* * *

I go home twice during my dad's six-month cancer treatment process. Twice—that's it. Avoidance is my language. The first time I go home is the weekend he is having surgery to remove the cancer. The night before I drive back home, I stay out late drinking and end up hooking up with one of my ex-boyfriend's best friends. I am in the middle of a shame spiral, and I don't know how to get out. I wake up at 6:00 a.m.—but I am hung over and have a man in my bed. Ugh. I get out of bed and pack my bags for my trip home and drive him home. I don't even remember his name. I drop him off and am hopeful I will never see him again. Please let me just erase that from my memory. I pull the Adderall out of my purse pocket and grab four 30 mg XRs. I grab a bottle of water and swallow them down. I need to be awake. I need to be alert. I need to focus on my dad's surgery.

I get to Huntsville just in time—literally, my parents are packing the car for the hospital stay. I pull into the driveway and throw my bag into the car. It is time to face reality. I need to come out of denial and be strong. I am the one who everyone relies on for strength. I assume my usual role as the strong one and power through the weekend.

My sister calls me crying about my dad's cancer and so does my mom—I know someone has to hold it all together—and that is going to be me. I am always the normal one, the strong one. The first year I moved to Lexington, my sister called me bawling her eyes out. "Mom told me I was fat and that I can't go to prom," she said through her tears. Apparently, she and my mom had gotten into an argument while dress shopping. The pain in my sister's voice was too much to bear. I hung up the phone with my sister and immediately called my mom. "How could you call Frankie that? What are you thinking?" I screamed. After she told me her side of the story—I didn't know which side was right-side up. "Well, you need to apologize to Frankie," I ordered. I called Frankie back, "Well, you need to call mom and apologize." They both listened because I always call the shots.

My dad makes it through the surgery. I barely make it through. I am almost out of Adderall, so I end up sleeping and visiting the snack machine and smoking cigarettes. I'm pretty sure I have eaten enough snacks for everyone in the waiting room—and there are a lot of people.

That's how I cope. I am almost out of Adderall—so I need to ration what I have remaining over the next few days. The less Adderall in my system, the hungrier I am. Plus—I need something to cope with my feelings of death and abandonment and chaos—so food is the most readily available resource. And boy do I use it. I gain five pounds in three days. Food is how I numb my experience. It's how I make it through my dad's hospital stay. It's how I manage my mom and my sister's feelings. It's how I "deal" with it all.

My second visit home during my dad's cancer scare is during his chemo treatment. The evening of my dad's chemo treatment my mom gets really drunk. I am in the kitchen when I discover her sneaking a drink. She looks me in the eyes, and I know she has been drinking. There's something about her eyes—maybe from childhood—that is so familiar. Her eyes are squinted and they are gray and cloudy and lifeless. It reminds me of the holidays. Frankie and I would wake up so excited for Christmas. We'd run down the stairs to find our presents—hers were always on the brown leather chair and ottoman and mine were on the right side of the couch. Our gifts were displayed so thoughtfully—and our stockings overflowed with all the necessities—shampoo, conditioner, deodorant, bath bombs. Joy of a sober Christmas morning would last an hour or so. My mom would wonder off into another room, but we were all too distracted with presents to notice. She would walk back into the main room, her eyes squinted and cloudy. "Let me help you open that present, Vitale," she would say aggressively. "No, mom, I'm fine. I got it," I would respond. "Fine then. It's not like your father and I don't do everything for you girls," she would snap back. Her anger and her eyes and her criticisms.

My mom's eyes are no different during this visit home. "Mom, do you really need to be drinking right now when Dad needs us?" I say. My words are covered in resentment and anger. There's a long pause. Everything in my life is out of control. Can't she just get it together? Why does she have to drink? Can't she just stay sober while I'm home for a few days. Can't she be the adult, the parent? She grabs me hard by both arms and looks me directly in the eyes. "It's your turn to be the strong one," she says. "I'm off duty this weekend—it's your turn." If course, it's my fucking turn. It's always my fucking turn. I know deep down this is what I could expect. My heart sinks. I just want to be the child. I don't want to be the parent. I don't want to be the adult. I want to be comforted; I don't want to do the comforting. But I step up because that's what I do. And that's what I did. I play the adult and the parent all weekend. While my mom is off duty, I am on duty. This role reversal is all too familiar to me. Playing the adult is second nature. I basically came out of the womb as a forty-year-old.

I immerse myself in my work. Working twelve- and thirteen-hour days to keep my mind off reality. I go through several men during the next few months, all to numb the pain of the past, present, and future. I just want to be loved. I want someone to care about me. I want someone to love me. My parents' lives are consumed with my dad's cancer treatment and enabling my sister. Frankie is struggling in junior college. Her drug use has advanced from pot to pills, and she is unstable. She is using my parents for money, and they are really vulnerable right now, so it works. I am last on the list. Always last. They even forget to call me on my birthday. I just want someone, anyone, to pay attention to me, to notice me. My partying and drinking get worse, my Adderall tolerance increases, and I allow more men into my bedroom.

I have been at my current job for about three years and I am ready for a change. Because of my Adderall use, I am able to work a full-time job, while also being involved in the community full time. This gains me exposure and press and awards and gets me noticed by several different companies. I interview for three different jobs, two nonprofits and a law firm. I feel on top of the world in my professional life. I am being courted by different organizations—so at least I have my professional life together. After a half-dozen interviews, I end up taking a job as the marketing director of a law firm with 150 lawyers. I am only twenty-five years old.

* * *

There are many parallels in my life. As my dad's cancer goes into remission, so does my promiscuity. I have a new job and a new relationship. My life is steady—finally. I feel like I have it all together. Except that the demands of the new job also require more Adderall. My tolerance starts climbing—I am up to 210–240 mg XR a day—that is three 30 mg XRs first thing in the morning, and three 30 mg XRs in the afternoon, and one or two more in the evening. I work from 8:00 a.m. until 3:00 or 4:00 a.m. every day of the week. The demands of the job and my ambitions are unrealistic, and I expect perfection from myself. And Adderall gives me that. My friends see how hard I am working, and all my professional achievements, and they ask me, "How do you have the energy to work that many hours?" And I respond with "It comes naturally, I guess." Which is total bullshit.

I am cheating the system. I am cheating everyone around me. And I am lying. I am lying about my addiction. I am a fucking liar. I am working so many hours that some nights I don't even go to sleep—I am too afraid that I won't wake up in the morning—which has happened a few times before. I stay up so late working that by the time I finally get to bed—3:30 or 4:00 a.m., I sleep through my alarm and am late to work. And my solution to that is to skip going to bed—which is messed up. My solution should have been to stop taking Adderall, but let's be real—that isn't an option.

My increased tolerance to Adderall means an increased need for it. What normally gets me through the month now only gets me through the first two weeks of the month. I talk to Dr. 3 about increasing my dosage because of the demands of my job, hoping to appeal to her age, as she is old enough to be my grandmother and would hopefully see it that way and feel bad for me. She increases the dosage from two 30 mg XRs a day to three 30 mg XRs a day—but that still isn't enough. I am calling at least once a month to say that I have lost a prescription or misplaced it. (Fun fact; no one in the history of addiction "loses" a prescription.) But my doctor is falling for my games and manipulation and she replaces my prescriptions upon my request.

I am filling certain prescriptions under insurance at one pharmacy and filling other prescriptions without insurance and paying cash at other pharmacies. I know which pharmacists treat me as a drug seeker, and which ones don't care. I am three years into my Adderall addiction—I have been caught doctor shopping by a pharmacist before, and I will never go back to that pharmacy again, and thankfully they never pursue me or press charges. I am not going to allow that to happen again. I am a pro now—I am seeing Dr. 3, and I am using four pharmacies to fill my prescriptions. I am in a rhythm—an Adderall rhythm. I get a prescription from my doctor and determine which pharmacy to use. Thirty days have to pass since my last fill at any of the pharmacies, so it is all a game to me. I know the exact schedule of all my pharmacies—which ones will allow me to fill a few days in advance, and which ones think I am sneaky. One time I try a new pharmacy—I am desperate. I have completely run out of Adderall, and none of my other prescriptions are ready to fill—it hasn't been thirty days. I decide to take one of my post-dated prescriptions and change the date. It says "09/12/2007" and I change the nine to an eight. The act of changing the date gives me anxiety, and it can also get me arrested and jail time if I am caught, but my hunger for Adderall is stronger than my anxiety.

As soon as I pull into the pharmacy parking lot, I feel a twinge of excitement and anxiety. The thought alone of filling my prescription gives me a high. I walk into the pharmacy—my hands shaking and my body tense. I am afraid of being rejected or caught. *What if they find out I am an addict? What if they know I am filling other prescriptions at other pharmacies? What will happen to me? Will I get arrested? How will I function without Adderall? What will people think?*

I turn my mind to something else. I am not ready to deal with my problem. I push it down. Every time it is my turn to speak to the pharmacist, I make small talk with them: "I love your glasses." "Ya'll must be busy today." "Your earrings are so cute." The small talk is my twisted way of distracting them from my addiction. I think that if I can engage them in conversation and seem likeable, then they will be more likely to fill my prescription. It is this sick and twisted game of manipulation that I play. *Don't appear drug seeking, Vitale,* I say to myself. *Talk to the pharmacist, avoid eye contact, be likeable.* I guess it works—who knows. After they take my prescription slip, then comes the waiting. Sometimes it takes twenty minutes, sometimes it takes hours. And I am willing to wait. In fact, so much of my life during this time is spent waiting. Waiting in a doctor's office, waiting on a prescription, waiting, waiting, waiting. If I am not working or drinking, then I am waiting on Adderall. I wait on the benches in the pharmacy, or I wait outside in my car and smoke—sometimes I do both. I am sweating while I am waiting—just hoping that their system doesn't flag me as a drug addict. I hope and pray and ask God for forgiveness—"just one more prescription, God. Just one more."

I let nothing stand in my way of my Adderall. I show up late, postpone meetings, reschedule appointments if they interfere with obtaining and filling another prescription. This means I am out of the office a lot getting the drug. But it doesn't matter. I make up for it with the all-nighters I am pulling almost every weeknight.

I am excelling at my job and getting high off the praise. My worth is defined by my professional success, my salary, and my social life. I expect perfection from myself in all areas of my life, and I achieve it. The more Adderall I take, the more I accomplish at work and the higher my salary climbs. And the higher my salary climbs, the better I feel about myself—plus, I can afford my Adderall habit.

I work closely with the managing partner of the law firm, Tom. He is smart and funny and attractive and powerful. He includes me on strategic initiatives of the firm and high-level decision-making. I hold a lot of power and influence for a twenty-something marketing director, and I thrive off it. There are rumors going around the firm that Tom and I are in a relationship, but it isn't true. We are together a lot, but he is married with three kids, although, I have seen him out with other women from time to time. However, my fondness for him turns into an attraction. I look forward to seeing him in the office and working with him on projects. I plan my outfits for work to make sure I look good. Tom is twenty-seven years my senior, but I am attracted to him anyway. It never goes further than that. We never cross the line. Until we do.

Eighteen months after working together, our professional relationship turns into a personal relationship. Tom starts sending me texts that are flirtatious and inquisitive and intriguing. I want more. I know I am crossing the line—and I like it. Nothing good can come of this. But the excitement and the chaos and the drama draw me in. He invites me to dinner the next week, and I know it is more than a work dinner—I know it could possibly lead to something risky. And I go anyway. I want to be chased. I am attracted to him and he is forbidden.

I arrive at the restaurant and find him at the bar. He is drinking a martini and looks so good in his Zegna suit and Hermes tie. I am drawn to his power and our connection and the danger. I sit down next to him and order a bourbon and ginger ale. We talk about work and strategy and laugh about people at work. I'm sitting close to him and my body is turned toward him and his is turned toward mine. My body feels high on lust and butterflies and pheromones. I'm four or five bourbons in, and the restaurant begins closing and we're the only two people left. He turns to me and we lock eyes. "Can I kiss you?" he asks. It is a rhetorical question. I look around to see if there's anyone we know, and before I answer, he kisses me. I feel a rush of excitement and rebellion. I stop him mid kiss and say it's a bad idea. And he leans in to kiss me again. And I let him. He ends up coming to my house and we can barely keep our hands off each other and we have sex.

I wake up the next morning, and I'm hung over. I call in sick to work because I can't believe what I just did. I'm too consumed with guilt and shame to be at work. *I can't believe I slept with my married, older boss. What the fuck was I thinking? What have I done? What have I started? How did I let this happen?* I immediately want to take it all back. I want to take back the dinner and the kissing and the flirting and the sex. Tom is seeing other women, too. And I am friends with one of the other women. So not only have I become a home wrecker, I have also chosen a guy over a friend. Who the fuck do I think I am? How did I get here? I go into my living room to find my phone and I have two missed texts—one from my best friend Meghan asking me how last night went, and the other from Tom asking if he can have lunch with me. I don't know how to respond to either text. I've just blown up my entire world and I don't know what to think or what to do. I don't know how to put it all back together.

FOUR

Adderall Intermission

The weeks turn into months. Tom comes over two or three nights a week and occasionally one weekend night. He can't stay over because he is married. Every time he leaves my house I feel like a slut, a mistress, a home wrecker. We are crazy in love, but we are also crazy. We do not think anything through.

Before Tom, I only drank on the weekends, but now I am drinking every day. Because my mom is an alcoholic, I know it is dangerous to drink every day, but it also helps me forget about the fact that I am dating my married boss. It also makes me forget that I am lying to all my friends and isolating them. The more I drink, the more I can forget my shame and the more I can pretend that what I am doing with Tom doesn't bother me.

Tom is married with three kids, and he is dating several other women. My ultimatum to him is that he has to separate from his wife and separate from the other women. It can only be me and him, or I am out. And I mean it. He believes me, and after only a few months of dating me, he moves out of his house. He also ends things with the other women—at least that's what he tells me.

The first six or eight months of our relationship are dangerous and secretive and exciting. I am addicted to the excitement. I am addicted to his power and his attraction to me. I love feeling wanted. I love being the adored twenty-seven-year old of my fifty-four-year-old boss. I feel sexy and powerful. I eat it all up. I lose more weight during this time, not because of my Adderall use, but because I am overcome with anxiety that comes from living a secret and a lie. I am in love and I can't tell anyone. I am in love, and we can't even go out in public together. If someone from the law firm sees us together as a couple, or one of our friends sees us, our lives and our careers will be destroyed.

Since we can't go out in public as a couple where we live, we travel. We travel to Bermuda and Charleston and Chicago and Boston. Travel is our only escape. It is the only safe space where we can be ourselves in public. And it feels exciting and fun and luxurious. One of my closest childhood friends is getting married in Boston, so Tom joins me for a few days before the wedding. He can't go with me to the wedding because I didn't respond for two people—no one knows we are dating. He leaves the day of my friend's wedding, and the pit in my stomach and loneliness are more than I can bear. I end up telling me friend I have an emergency and I book an earlier flight home and miss her wedding. I miss my friend's wedding.

At work we play our same roles—he as the managing partner and me as the marketing director. In fact, we make sure that I receive no special treatment. I even miss my annual raise because we want to be extra certain that if work does find out, they won't think I am getting special treatment. It is complete insanity. And I love it. I love the rush of the drama and the secrets and the hiding. I love the excitement. I abandon myself and my needs for Tom and the relationship. I become willing to risk it all—risk everything I have worked so hard for—for him.

I need to normalize my life as much as possible in the midst of my relationship chaos. I walk into the grocery to buy the ingredients for my favorite meal—pita dip. It's red onion, Roma tomatoes, feta, and black olives mixed with olive oil and balsamic vinegar, and then I eat it with freshly baked pita bread. It's my favorite and it reminds me of home. I have everything I need except the pita, so I walk into the bakery section. I get a call and it's Frankie. My heart sinks—what does she want now? "Hey, Lolly," she says as if we're best friends. "I have really good news to share with you." I know what she's going to say before she even tells me. "I'm pregnant with a baby boy and we're due June 28." She doesn't even have a job or a place to live, how is she expecting to bring a child into this world? And her new husband is basically a drug dealer. "Um, congratulations," I say hesitantly. I fake a smile over the phone. I knew this was going to happen; it was only a matter of time. But now? Really? "We are so excited, and we've even picked out his name—it's Bentley." I'm going to be an aunt. Great. I leave the grocery store and when I get home, I realize I forgot to buy the pita bread. I can't believe this is happening.

Tom gets a divorce and his deposition triggers the word getting out. He is deposed and admits to our affair and after that everyone at the law firm finds out and our lives and our relationship are forever changed. The day the news comes out at work, Tom is working in the Louisville office and I am working in the Lexington office. I have to face the judgment and the looks and the comments all by myself. I get on the elevator and push the button for the twentieth floor. A few other attorneys are ushered in before the doors close, and they all look at me with disdain. I am no longer the successful marketing director; I am now the woman who is having an affair with her married, older boss. They are looking at me as a cliché—the young woman who sleeps her way up the corporate ladder. I feel so much judgment and shame. My mind has a million thoughts moving around in it: *I'm a slut who sleeps with her boss; of course this happened—what did I think was going to happen?; the successful resume and career I've built have now been erased.* I am standing in the elevator; my entire body is tense and I feel the weight of the world on my shoulders. I feel the weight of my affair on my shoulders. I have enough shame and judgment for myself that I don't need anyone else's. My perfect love affair is no longer perfect.

My Adderall use during this time only exasperates the circumstances. I become manic about my career and the potential consequences and fallout. With perfection, I want everything to be wrapped up in a pretty package. I want to solve things immediately so I can move on. That isn't the case with this. We can't just move on. I take more Adderall to focus on work, and I drink more bourbon to numb my reality. My Adderall addiction and my drinking and my relationship create the perfect storm of chaos and excitement and dread. And my Adderall tolerance is increasing and the prescriptions from Dr. 3 aren't cutting it. The growing tension in my life creates a growing need for Adderall. I start seeing a fourth doctor to keep up with my Adderall habit. I can't find an opening with a psychologist, so I find a family practitioner. I go to my first appointment—Dr. 4 is young and naïve. I will definitely be able to manipulate her.

Tom is forced to step down from his role as managing partner—which is completely demoralizing for him. He stays at the law firm, but he is no longer the boss—he is now a regular attorney. I feel like it is all my fault. And he feels like it is all my fault, too. He is angry and ashamed and demoralized. He feels like people should understand our love—but that's not the real world. The real world judges us for dating someone in the workplace and breaking up a marriage. And at this point, I don't really disagree. If it was someone else in my position, I would be judging them, too. I am judging me. Tom blames me for losing his job. He feels like a failure at work and he feels like a failure for ending his marriage. We should be excited that the news is out—we should be excited to finally go out in public and celebrate our love. But it is tainted. We are worn out from the years of hiding our romance—nothing plays out the way we thought it would. We are good at working together and that is now taken away—I am no longer allowed to report to him, and I am assigned a new boss, the new managing director.

The bright spot in all of this is that no one ever doubts my work ethic because I get results, so I am not treated differently on that level. Plus—people blame Tom for the relationship more than me. They think it is an abuse of power. I don't see it that way, but it doesn't matter. In the end, I receive the better deal. People treat me the same, but they treat Tom much differently. And that drives a bigger wedge in our relationship. I am still enjoying my job and he is emasculated.

Our relationship starts running on autopilot. We spend the same amount of time together—maybe even more time together—but we aren't communicating. We merely exist. We inhabit the same space, but we aren't connected. We are disconnected. We go through the motions—he exercises after work and I am in my Adderall work haze and then we discuss dinner plans. He drinks several martinis and I drink several bourbons and we sit down to eat dinner while watching TV, buzzing from the alcohol. Then we go to bed and sleep on different sides. We are together, but we aren't. We are unable to bridge our pain. We each see our own pain as more important than the other's pain. And the weight of our own pain is too much for each of us to bear.

Tom only ever knew me as an Adderall addict. I mean, he doesn't know I am abusing Adderall—but that's the only version of me he knows. The Adderall version of Vitale is who he fell in love with. Not the version of me underneath all of the Adderall—hell, I don't even know what that version of me is like. In the moments when I am nearing empty on my Adderall bottle, the tension will rise in our relationship. The amount of Adderall in my bottle is a direct reflection of our relationship. When I have just filled a prescription, our relationship is full. We laugh and kiss and make love and act like we did when we first started dating. When my Adderall bottle is almost empty, so is our relationship. I pick fights, distance myself from Tom, and create drama. I drink too much and find the reasons why we shouldn't be together. "The only thing we have in common is work," I jab at him. "I don't even know why we're together. You're never going to introduce me to your kids. We have too much crap between us now for this to work."

* * *

Now that I am seeing Dr. 3 and Dr. 4, I am getting two to three prescriptions a month—but it isn't enough. I am faking a misplaced or lost prescription once a month—alternating between Drs. 3 and 4. And when that doesn't work, I change the date on my post-dated prescriptions from Dr. 3. I can't do that with Dr. 4 because she only gives me one prescription at a time—and they are electronically printed—so I can't change the date on them. It is risky behavior. Each time I call one of the doctor's offices, I am anxious, thinking, *What should I say? What lie should I use this time? Will I get caught?*

I am afraid of getting caught but I am more afraid of running out of Adderall. I play this cat-and-mouse game with the doctors for a few months. Then one day I push the limit. I call Dr. 4 and request an early refill—it is the first week of January and I make the excuse about work travel and being out of town to visit family. I want to "make sure I don't run out while I am out of town." Total lie. But I think it is a good one. I leave a message with the receptionist. And I don't hear back for two days.

* * *

I get news that my mother's older sister, Valary, is in critical condition. Her Lou Gehrig's disease is about to take her life. She was diagnosed eighteen months ago, and since I live remotely, I am able to pretend it isn't happening. But I can't ignore it any longer. She is going to die. My mother's younger sister Catheryn calls me to tell me that I need to head home to Alabama because Valary only has a few more days to live. Valary lives in the same city as my parents, Huntsville. And my mom, the expert martyr that she is, has become Valary's caretaker. It has been painful hearing my mother's retelling of all the stories and pity parties over the past months. I spend my time on the phone with her tuning her out, just wishing that the drama would die so I could move on.

I am torn. *Do I wait to hear back from my doctor to get my refill or do I drive home now?* The pressure to go home eventually wins. I have enough Adderall to last me a week, and then hopefully the other prescription will be ready for me when I get back. I have been on the road for two hours when Dr. 4 finally returns my call. I always screen doctor's calls. My protocol is to let them leave a message so I can gauge beforehand whether they might comply with a new prescription or not. Always on the defensive, waiting for someone to "catch" me doctor shopping, I rationalize that I can tell whether the call is good or bad by the tone in their voicemail. I never want to be surprised. I can control my response in case I get caught doctor shopping or forging prescription dates. The message from Dr. 4 is longer than most voicemails I have received from other doctors. My heart starts racing. A long voicemail probably isn't good news. I pick up my phone and take a deep breath. I don't know what the message will say. I press play on the message and put my phone up to my ear. My hands are sweating. "Hi Vitale, I'm Rachel the office manager, and I'm calling to let you know that we will no longer serve as your doctor. When you continued to call and request prescriptions of Adderall, I grew suspicious. You need to call me back at your earliest convenience. This is an urgent matter."

Holy fuck. My heart races. I grip the steering wheel with both hands, as if I am driving through a torrential downpour. Scary thoughts begin racing in my mind: *What if she called the police? Is she going to tell Dr. Three? What am I going to do? Fuck, fuck, fuck.*

I take the last puff of my cigarette and I throw it out the window. I need to return the call. "Hello, this is Vitale Buford. Can I please speak to Rachel?" my voice rattles. There are a million different ways this conversation can end, and none of them are positive.

"Hi, Vitale. This is Rachel the office manager. You are in trouble young lady," she says like a principal reprimanding me in detention. "You are seeing multiple doctors for Adderall. We will no longer provide you with health care, and I am calling Dr. 3 to inform her of what you are doing. I am faxing her your report of filled prescriptions." My Adderall career is about to end. I don't know how to feel or what to do. My chest tightens and I grip the steering wheel so hard that I leave sweat stains on it. I can't breathe. *How am I going to handle this? What am I going to do?* My body is physically in the car, but my mind is somewhere else. I turn the music off because I need silence to help me handle the chaos. I need to think, but I can't think. I can't do anything except pull over at the next rest stop and gag. I open the car door and step outside. The cold air feels good against my skin. *How is this happening to me? Why did I have to be so greedy?* My life is over.

The rest of my drive home is a blur. When I arrive in Huntsville, I'm expecting a call from Dr. 3 at any moment. She should have received the files by now and she's going to be pissed and cut off my Adderall supply. My mind is far away from the important issue—Aunt Valary. All I can think about is my future and that it's in my doctor's hands. She could turn me into the police, she could do anything she wanted to do—she has the power.

I walk into my parent's house and my phone rings. And my heart stops. Here it goes. I don't let this call go to voicemail—I know what it's about. I know what's going to happen. I answer the phone and it's Dr. 3's receptionist—I have always liked her because I am always able to pull one over on her. But not now. "Hi, Vitale. Dr. 3 wants to see you immediately—it's an urgent issue. Are you available tomorrow?" she asks.

"I'm actually in Alabama; my aunt is dying. I won't be back until next week," I explain. I'm sure she doesn't believe me. Why would she? Now I am pegged not only as an addict but as a liar because the two always go hand in hand.

"Well, I'm sorry to hear that," she says with disregard. "The doctor has an opening on Monday afternoon at 4:00 p.m. Will that work?"

"Yes, that should work. I will see you then." Fuck. My mind should be on my aunt and my family, but it's not—my mind is on my Adderall.

* * *

I'm stressing about the consequences of my doctor shopping now that my cover has been blown, and I am stressing about the scene I will find at the hospital, where the whole family—including my sister—will be surrounding my Aunt Valary. I don't want to face my family. They are so predictable. I know before I even get there that my mom and sister will be acting overly dramatic about it all—and I can't stand that shit. I can see it now: everyone crying over my aunt's hospital bed, my mom sobbing while sitting in the chair next to her, and my sister standing at the foot of the bed with my dad just observing it all, sitting in the chair in the corner of the room. It's too damn much.

I feel sorry for my Aunt Valary, as she doesn't have many friends and lives a pretty secluded life, so there probably won't be many people mourning her. Everyone will be looking at me to make the decisions—should we wait in the hospital room until she dies, or should we go home and wait? As if I have the answers. I want to avoid all of it just like I did with my dad's cancer. I stop myself from thinking about it. I focus on my Adderall crisis instead.

I get to the hospital and locate my aunt's room. I'm not ready to be the strong one—the one in charge—the one everyone is looking to for strength. I'm not ready to pretend I didn't just get cut off from Adderall, and could potentially be facing serious legal consequences. But I don't have a choice. I take a deep breath before I walk into Valary's hospital room. "Vitale, we are so glad you're finally here," my mom says. "We've been waiting for you." Her eyes are cloudy and her speech is slurred; she must be drinking. She reaches out to hug me, but I don't want to be touched.

Clearly, no one is in control right now. I walk over to my dad to see if he knows what's going on. "The nurse says it may be a few more days and we can go ahead and go home if we want," he says. I make the executive decision for all of us to go back to the house.

My mom is being overly emotional. We all go home for a few hours and I take a shower and obsess over my doctor's appointment the following week. I go downstairs after my shower and my mom is completely drunk. *How did this happen in the span of forty-five minutes?* Or—a better question is—why does this always happen? She can't cope with her sister's death, so she gets wasted. And now the attention is on her. Of course. This is such bullshit. It reminds me of when my dad had cancer, or when my grandmother had cancer. My mom milks it for all it's worth. It's just another excuse for her to drink. Honestly, it could be a normal Tuesday and that's a good enough excuse for her to drink.

"Mom, is this really the appropriate time to be drinking?" I snap at her. I look to my father to be a voice of reason, and whisper to him, "Dad, seriously—how could you let mom drink at a time like this?" I don't want my mom to hear our conversation. And then there's my sister—she is bawling her eyes out while on the phone with whomever she's dating at this moment and ignoring her son Bently who is in the playpen. He's seven months old now and it's only the second time I've met him. The first time was a week after he was born last year. It's a complete cluster fuck. Everyone at home is playing the victim. No one is taking control. No one is leading us. So, I'll lead.

The hospital calls with the update that my aunt's condition has drastically worsened and we need to get down there immediately. My mother, father, Frankie, and Aunt Catheryn go into Aunt Valary's room to say their goodbyes. I'm the last one. Flashes of her disease run through my mind and I think of how terrible this has been. I give her a hug and kiss her forehead. I don't know what to think or say—it's almost like I'm being watched by everyone else. I step out of the room and she dies. It's almost like she was holding on until I said goodbye.

* * *

The rest of the weekend I'm distracted. My mind is consumed by the million different ways my Adderall career can end. And then there's my family drama. My mom is drunk. "I can't believe my sister is gone," she sobs. And then there's Frankie outside smoking and she has her phone pressed between her right shoulder and her right ear, talking to who knows. Her eyes are cloudy, too; she must be on pain pills or benzos. I can tell when she's really messed up—her voice gets high-pitched and she acts overly nice to cover up the fact that she's fucked up. And then there's my dad—he's isolating in his favorite spot, the garage, pretending my mom and my sister aren't messed up. And I'm stuck watching Bentley because no one else is—and I don't even like kids.

Nearly everyone who sees Bentley gawks at him and says how great babies are at seven months old. He is at the "cute and cuddly and fun" stage, according to everyone, except I don't see it. I'm not into Bentley—it hurts too much. And I don't know what to do with kids anyway. Maybe it's because I've always been an adult—who knows. And there's been so much chaos surrounding his little life—he's only seven months old, but it has been seven months of chaos. Frankie and her drug dealing, addict husband stayed with my parents for a little while, then his parents, then who knows. They've gone from place to place to place. And they've left Bentley with my parents for weeks while Frankie disappears on a bender, only to return and rip the baby away from them for weeks. I've been afraid to love him. I've been afraid to get in the middle of it. The fact that my whole family is easily ruining their own lives is one thing, but a little innocent helpless human being? What they could potentially do to him is scary and way too big, too big for me to want to look closely at it. I've avoided having a relationship with him, to stay out of it and to avoid thinking about it. And aside from the chaos, I've never been a huge fan of kids; they annoy me. They require too much care and attention. And I don't have that to give. I don't need needy.

But here I am stuck with Bentley. And I need to take him home because it's his bedtime. I don't even know how to work his car seat and it's giving me anxiety. And no one is around for me to ask because they are all consumed with Valary's death. I'm impacted by her death, too, but no one gives a fuck. "Here, Vitale, you take Bentley. We all need to mourn and drink and be pathetic." I figure out the car seat situation as best as possible and I lock him in safely. We both lock eyes—I'm foreign to him. He doesn't trust me. He doesn't trust anyone.

I start the car and he starts crying. I move my arm behind my seat, and I grab his little hand in mine, and he stops crying. His little seven-month-old hand is holding onto my pinkie finger from the backseat. I drive the entire way home like that. I put Bentley to sleep in his crib and it's much easier than I anticipated. People always talk about the horrors of getting their kids to sleep. But this is pretty easy.

I walk into the guest room of my parents' house to get ready for bed. It has been a long day. I start undressing and I fall to my knees. I don't know how I'm going to fix my Adderall dilemma. I don't know what the consequences will be for me. Tears of stress stream down my face. I climb into bed and Bentley starts crying. I don't know how to handle this. *Why did they put me in charge of Bentley—I don't know what I'm doing.* I go into his room and he's sitting up and crying. I pick him up and hold him tight and rock him back and forth. He stops crying and instead of putting him back into his crib, I bring him back into my bedroom. I hold him tight in my arms and he looks at me, this time with trust. I didn't know it was possible for me to love him, but I do.

* * *

Back home in Lexington, I'm nervous the night before my appointment with Dr. 3. Maybe I will have a few extra drinks tonight to calm my nerves. I need to get some rest. I'm at Tom's house because we're in a mindless routine of staying together every night—it's not healthy or balanced, but I don't want to think about it. And tonight, I don't want to be alone—I'm too afraid of what tomorrow might bring. I need a distraction. Tom can tell something is off, but he doesn't ask. He has no idea that his girlfriend is an Adderall addict and that I've been lying to him. I am afraid if he knows, he would leave me. I pour myself a bourbon and ginger ale.

It's Monday, January 8, 2012. There are a million different ways it can play out this afternoon—and none of them are positive. I feel so alone and sad. No one knows about my addiction except for my doctors—how will everyone around me respond? Will Tom still love me? Do I even have to tell him?

I pull into the parking lot of Dr. 3's office and my heart is pounding—in fact, my whole body is pounding. I take the elevator to the second floor and walk to the end of the hallway to her office. I've been seeing Dr. 3 for two years—it's a long-term relationship—and she's about to break up with me. My drug dealer is about to end things, and I'm scared. I check in with the receptionist, Barb—she's the one I always call when I "lose" a prescription and need a replacement. She was always there for me and now I've betrayed her. "I will let Dr. Three know you're here," she says. She has a look in eyes that says, "Girl, you are in big trouble." It's the same look I got when the pharmacist caught me filling two prescriptions. The reception area used to feel warm, and now it feels cold and lonely. There is nobody here on my side. I sit down and wait an entire hour.

I sit down in my usual spot on Dr. 3's couch. And she sits down in her chair across from me. Her prescription pad is sitting on the table next to her, but she won't need it today. "Vitale, you have an addiction," she says. She pauses and waits for my reaction. Except I have no reaction; my face is frozen. "And instead of cutting you off and leaving you in the cold, I want to help you get sober. I will no longer be prescribing you Adderall, except to titrate you off it." *Well, at least she's not going to call the police.* "I hope you understand the severity of the situation." Then her compassionate tone turns stern. "This needs to be addressed and taken seriously."

"Yes ma'am," I respond, my head turned to the floor. "I understand I have a problem." Tears start swelling up in my eyes. I hadn't expected to say such a thing out loud, and there it is, and I know I won't do a damn thing about it. I'm not ready to stop Adderall, but I have no choice. I've been found out and there's nowhere else to turn. "I also think you need to consider outpatient treatment to help you get sober," she adds. The word treatment freaks me out. I don't have that bad of a problem—outpatient treatment sounds a bit extreme. My biggest concern is weight gain—what am I going to do to maintain my weight? I'm going to get fat and ugly without Adderall. Fuck.

"During the time you come off Adderall it will be important to have a support system in place," she says. "Is there anyone that can help you during this time?" Ugh. I don't want anyone to know about this, but I guess she's right.

"My boyfriend, Tom, could help," I say reluctantly. "He doesn't know about my addiction, but I can tell him."

"Good," she says. "I want you to bring him with you tomorrow and I will go over the detoxing process."

"Okay, thank you," I respond.

"Also, Vitale, I'm retiring and closing my practice at the end of next month, so you will need to find another doctor to support you in this journey after my retirement," she adds. Well—that's interesting. At least I don't have to face this after she retires. For now, I need to face Tom.

* * *

That evening Tom comes over and I'm already on my second bourbon. I need to calm down—my body is so tense, and my mind is racing, and I need alcohol to make it better. I need to numb the pain. He walks in the door and I dive straight into what I need to talk about. There's no hesitation. I wear my emotions on my sleeve, and I've never had a poker face. "I need to tell you something really serious," I say to open the conversation.

"Okay," he says. He looks confused. He has no idea what's about to hit him.

"I have an Adderall addiction and I need to get sober," I say quickly. The words fall out of my mouth. "I've been struggling with this for several years and it's become a problem. I need to address it and I need your help. My doctor said it would best if you support me during this time. And she wants you to come to my appointment with her tomorrow."

I don't leave any space for him to respond or think or consider. It's all about me. He's in shock, but he wants to help me—he wants to understand. He doesn't even know what Adderall is, so I explain it to him. "I started using Adderall in college to help me with school and I continued using it and now it has gotten out of control. And I have a problem," I explain. I want him to understand—but only on my terms. I want him to understand the severity of it all—but not really. What can I tell him that will make him feel like I'm being honest? I don't want him to know about my body image issues or that I use Adderall to control my weight. I just want him to think I used it innocently in college and that it has become a problem—which is the truth. I want him to understand that I have a problem. All this information has just been dropped on me so suddenly. And I feel so alone and so scared. And I want to feel less alone—that's the main point of me telling him. "You know how I built the law firm's marketing department overnight? And how I would get those huge end of year reports to you in a few days?" I start explaining. "I was able to do that because of Adderall. And do you remember that time I was late to the partners' meeting and everyone was looking for me? It's because I slept through my alarm because the previous three nights I had stayed up until three or four in the morning working." He looks at me and takes a sip of his martini. "What is Adderall used for? How long have you been using it? Isn't it for people with ADHD?" He begins asking me all these questions like a lawyer would. He wants to know all the details. Tom has only known me on Adderall—so of course he's confused. He doesn't know me any other way.

Tom and I are in the waiting room of Dr. 3's office. The waiting area is different this time. I used to wait in anticipation of getting my new post-dated prescriptions. I used to get a high knowing that I would soon have more Adderall. It was all a game. This time is different—my Adderall days are over. Tom knows about my addiction now, and there is no going back. At least I won't be facing it alone. We walk back to her office and we both sit down on the couch. She waits until we are both situated. Tom makes a joke to lighten the mood, but I want nothing to do with it. I'm scared shitless—there's no joke in the world that would make this moment lighthearted for me. She explains the nature of my addiction to Tom and the severity. "Vitale has been abusing Adderall for quite some time now and she will need help tapering off the drug," Dr. 3 explains. "I'm not sure how much Vitale has told you."

"Well," I interject, "I've told him that I have a problem and that it started in college so I could study longer." I want to control the conversation, not

Dr. 3. I'm afraid of what she will reveal to him that I don't want her to reveal.

"Vitale has been getting Adderall from multiple sources and it has gotten out of control," she continues. "I think the main reason Vitale is on this is for weight management."

I'm caught off guard. I know it's true, but I don't want anyone else to know that—so I deny it. "No, I don't think that's right," I respond.

"What is Adderall used for? How does it impact her? How often is she taking it? And how do we get her off it?" Tom asks. He's always thorough. The two of them go back and forth with the question and answer portion of our meeting—it's as if they're in cahoots with each other. I tune out and look out the window at the gray sky, and it matches my mood.

Dr. 3 begins explaining the process of titrating me off Adderall. It will take ten days, and she wants Tom to be responsible for giving me the lower doses of Adderall. Great—now *Tom* is my drug dealer. "You may need further support for detoxing from Adderall and there is an outpatient program at the local rehab you should look into," Dr. 3 suggests. Rehab? No fucking way. I can't believe she's mentioning it again; my addiction isn't that bad. Rehab sounds scary. I'm perturbed and inconvenienced by all this. I didn't want anyone to know—and now Dr. 3, Barb, and Tom know. Dr. 3 writes three different prescriptions for different Adderall doses and hands them to Tom. Of course, she doesn't hand them to me. I can't be trusted. We leave her office with the prescriptions and we are both silent the whole way home.

I don't want to get off Adderall. I'm being forced into this—I'm pissed and resentful. I go along with it to make Tom and Dr. 3 happy. Maybe this is the right time. Maybe I need to grow up and live without Adderall. No—I don't want this. I'm not ready. I call the outpatient treatment center to inquire about their program and they don't have a treatment program for Adderall. Maybe I didn't explain it correctly? Dr. 3 told me there was a program, but I guess I misunderstood. I feel relieved that they don't have treatment to deal with my specific problem. I'm off the hook. Outpatient treatment is no longer an option. Check. Now that part of my dread can go away. Plus, I can do this by myself with Tom's help. I guess.

The first few days of my titration are normal because I still have a few pills left over from my last prescription, so I supplement it with my titrated amount. By day three, I'm solely on the titrated amount and I feel better than I expected. Maybe it's because I no longer have to lie about my addiction—I've kept it a secret for seven years, and now it's out in the open. Or maybe it's because I'm not doing it alone—Tom is helping me.

It's day ten coming off Adderall and the last day of my drug titration. Today I'm only prescribed to take one 5 mg of Adderall. Which is nothing—I was taking fifty times that amount. It's basically pointless to be taking it, but I comply because it's the right thing to do. It's what I'm supposed to do. I've started working out because I'm scared to death of gaining weight—and I've already gained eight pounds. Eight pounds in ten days. Fuck. I feel fat and ugly—just as I had anticipated. Tom and I never talk about Adderall again, unless I bring it up. I don't have anyone to talk to about it—no real support system or plan for sobriety. I don't even look at it as sobriety. I look at it as being off Adderall.

For three months, I attempt life without Adderall. I work out obsessively because of my body shame—I need to have the perfect body. Adderall quieted all my body talk and weight obsession, and it isn't quiet anymore. It is as loud as ever. My job performance is slacking—I have little motivation and I am tired all the time. I am still getting used to life sans Adderall. My friends find it interesting that I am working out all the time—this is unusual behavior for me. I didn't have to exercise with Adderall and so on the outside, it seemed as if I was naturally thin. But I am not—I have to work for it now. And it isn't working. No matter how much I exercise, I am still gaining weight—and it is affecting every other area of my life. I don't want to go out with my friends because I feel fat. I don't want to have sex with Tom because I feel fat and ugly. I don't want to go into the office because I am unmotivated. I don't want to do life without Adderall—it is too hard. Perfection is too hard to achieve without my drugs. With Adderall, perfection was effortless. I want my old life back.

I've had enough. I don't want to live this way anymore. Maybe enough time has passed, and I can get a new Adderall prescription from another doctor? Dr. 3 has retired so my former patient files are inaccessible. I can also use her retirement as the reason I'm looking for a new doctor. This could be the perfect excuse. I'm hopeful again. I make an appointments with a new doctor.

I walk into the reception area of Dr. 5's office. I fill out the new patient paperwork and return it to the receptionist. I get a high just thinking about the possibility of going back on Adderall again. I sit in one of the chairs until my name is called. I follow the doctor back to his office. We both sit down, and he wants to understand my background—my family history and my current life, all of it. I just want the damn prescription, but I play his game. I've done this many times before. I can tell he's going to prescribe me Adderall—I've been able to manipulate him into liking me and feeling sorry for me at the same time—which is the perfect combination—I have him exactly where I want him. I want him to hurry up, but he wants to know more about my family life. He keeps pressing and pressing. I don't typically talk about my family—I'm not sure what that has to do with me. I want Adderall, so I give him what he wants. "My mother is an alcoholic," I tell him. I've never said that out loud, never ever. It feels strange to say it—maybe I'm making a bigger deal out of it than I need to. She drinks a lot—maybe the word alcoholic is too extreme. "You probably have a lot of shame as a child of an alcoholic," he says. Shame? What does that have to do with anything? And what does that have to do with my mom and me? I don't get what he's saying, but it sticks with me. He finally writes me a prescription and asks me to come back in a month to evaluate.

I'm back in business. My Adderall addiction is back in full swing. I even end up running out of my month's supply in less than three weeks— of course—I thought I could use Adderall normally but that's not the case. I'm almost back to the same dosage as last time. It's like time never stopped. I'm back to my old routine in no time. I call Dr. 5 to replace my "lost" prescription. He agrees because he doesn't know my games yet. I don't ever want to run out of Adderall again. Never. I lose ten pounds in two weeks, which is perfect, because I'm going to the Kentucky Derby with Tom, and I need to fit into this dress I've been eyeing at one of the local boutiques. It feels good to be back to my old self at work and to be back in my old size two body. My intervention with Dr. 3 and Tom is a distant memory. I'm back in perfection mode and it feels good. I don't have to worry about weight gain or exhaustion or hunger or being unmotivated. Adderall gives me everything I need.

It's been one month since I've been taking Adderall again. And no one knows. I haven't told Tom—I'm surprised he can't tell—I'm a totally different person on it. This speaks to the bigger issue in our relationship—the fact that we are disconnected. The fact that we are merely existing alongside each other. We've been through so much together—an affair, a divorce, work drama, and my Adderall addiction—we are together out of obligation. It's a lot. If we can survive all those things together, then we are meant to be, right? I don't know. And I don't want to deal with it. And I don't want Tom to know that I'm back on Adderall, so I hide it from him. I've already put him through so much, plus—he wouldn't understand. He thinks I'm cheating the system by being on Adderall—that it's selfish of me. He doesn't get how deeply rooted this addiction is for me. And that the roots go way beyond Adderall. Way beyond.

It is summertime and I need more doctors to keep up with my Adderall tolerance. I can't believe it's taken no time at all to be back to my old dosage. I need multiple prescriptions and that requires multiple doctors. I really thought I would be able to take it as prescribed—but there's no way. I need more and more. I have appointments with two new doctors—Dr. 6 and Dr. 7 in the same week—I don't have time to waste and I'm back to playing my old games. Dr. 6 just needs an old Adderall bottle to prove the validity of my request. That's easy since I brought my extra bottle with me.

I go to Dr. 7's office and he prescribes it to me, no questions asked. Well—he asks if I can transfer my old doctor's files to him—and thank God they are locked away. Thank God I have an excuse. I don't want him to see the file because he will know—he will know everything: the doctor shopping, my illegal behavior, my addiction. Thank God he can't access those files. If he only knew. At the end of our session, he mentions to me that the laws in Kentucky are changing at the end of July and all doctors will now be required to pull patient records from the state's prescription database. *Shit.* This means he will be able to see if I'm seeing multiple doctors and filling multiple prescriptions. My other doctors will also be able to see the same thing. And this is happening in four weeks. I try to act calm and collected about it—I don't want to tip him off. I don't want him to figure out that I'm a drug seeker. I also need to figure out how I'm going to handle this.

The weeks pass and the law goes into effect. Dr. 5 and 6 refuse to write me prescriptions. Dr. 7 must have not pulled an entire prescription history because he doesn't seem to mind. He's still willing to see me. We have our second session and he writes me my second prescription. My other Adderall sources are cut off—I'm done. But at least I still have Dr. 7. Thank God. I fool myself into thinking I can handle just one prescription a month. I can do this—I can take my medicine as prescribed.

The weeks turn into months and it's fall. I'm still seeing my Dr. 7 and I'm still only getting one prescription per month. I wish there was some way around this. I wish I could get more Adderall. I'm not able to maintain my weight with this dosage. I'm not as productive at work. I'm hungry and tired like a normal person. I'm no longer perfect. But some Adderall is better than no Adderall.

FIVE

Addicted to Chaos

It's New Year's Eve. I'm cleaning my apartment manically and cooking appetizers for the party tonight. I look down at my phone and see text messages from an unknown number. "Is your last name still Buford?" it ominously says. Who could it be? I consider the day it is and why it would be significant for a stranger to contact me, prying into my personal life as if this person had some unwritten right to do so.

I look at the text again and remember the pact Jack and I made when we last saw each other. It was Christmas break two-and-a-half years ago back home in Alabama. We were drunk at 2:00 a.m. in my car listening to classic rock. We had met up accidentally at a mutual high school friend's party and began talking and flirting just like we had when we dated back in high school.

Seeing Jack was bittersweet. Not because he was my first kiss, my first serious boyfriend, and my first heartache, but because we shared a friendship with Matthew. Matthew was my best friend and my world, and he was Jack's best friend, too. Matthew was one year behind us in school—we met when I was a sophomore and he was a freshman. We had an instant connection, and instant fondness and affection for each other. And although we were never together romantically, he was my soul mate. And he was the only person who knew the real me—he made me feel safe and understood. We talked for hours on the phone every single night. My safety in the storm of high school hormones and my parents' unpredictability, Matthew had given me a sense of belonging. When everything else in my life was uncertain, he was my certainty. He was my source of light and love and understanding. He was always there for me, no matter what, until he wasn't. On June 7, 2000, Matthew died in a car accident. Jack was driving the car. Both of our lives were forever changed, and we were also trauma bonded.

Sitting in the car that drunken night, we listened to Lynyrd Skynyrd or Willie Nelson or Tom Petty. I could feel the attraction between us as we gazed into each other's eyes. You could cut the magnetism between us with a knife. We made a pact that if neither of us were married by the time we were thirty that we would marry each other. And both of us are now thirty and not married. So of course, this text message is from Jack!

I haven't seen Jack since that marriage pact, and now that I am with Tom, I force myself to stay away from the familiar pull I feel toward him. This has always been the pattern, since we left home for college. We go years without seeing or talking to each other (except for maybe a drunk text every now and then). I forget he even exists and then have intermittent spurts of longing for him. Longing for the excitement and chaos he brings to my life.

And then I get that motherfucking text from him. On New Year's Fucking Eve. Here it goes again. Here it starts. The butterflies in my stomach. The addiction to excitement and changes and newness. My addiction to the person I think he is.

Tom and I have been putting on fronts with each other for two-and-half years by this point, and I'm unhappy, so of course it's the perfect time for Jack to come running back into my life again. My addiction to excitement and perfection and Adderall is now complete with the validation and adoration and attention that Jack gives me.

"Who is this?" I respond. I am playing a coy game and he plays the waiting game, taking an hour to respond, leaving me with bated breath in the middle of my kitchen.

"You know who this is." The text says, calling my bluff.

So, I respond, waving a proverbial white flag of surrender, "Yes, my last name is still Buford."

Butterflies fill my stomach. How can someone feel so strongly for one person and be in a relationship with another? Are my feelings for Jack real? Are my feelings for Tom real? All I know is that it feels nice to be pursued. Tom hasn't been paying much attention to me lately and we're in a rut. Plus, all the drama unfolding from our affair really took it out of us. We have both turned away from each other instead of toward each other. We have made the problem him versus me, instead of us versus the problem. We don't communicate and we are like ships passing in the night. We spend time together, but it's simply out of routine. It's simply out of obligation. This way the absolute combustion of his life has not happened in vain.

Immediately, my phone rings and I see the Alabama area code 256. I know it's him. I get a rush of excitement and anxiety and I feel sixteen again. I answer the phone calmly and Jack says, "So . . . your last name is still Buford?" I can hear other voices in the background. He must be drunk at a party. I respond, "Yes, it is. How have you been?"

We talk about our plans for New Year's Eve and he says he'll call me in the next few days. I hang up the phone, and my entire body feels like it's on fire. I look in the mirror, and my cheeks are flushed, and my hands are shaking. I'm high on Adderall and this communication from Jack just makes me feel unstoppable. My life has been so boring and plain, and this is exactly the rush of excitement I need. I hate being bored, and my life has been so boring. Adderall and Jack make it exciting. This is exactly the feeling I've been missing—the adrenaline rush of lust and newness and butterflies.

I know exactly how things will play out when I let Jack into my life. But I'm also connected to him in a way that I'm not connected to anyone else. We experienced Matthew's death together. He's the only person who understands that part of my life. And he's the only person that knows that version of me: the pure, sixteen-year-old version of me. We know each other's families, and he knows the entire backstory with my sister and my mom. I don't have to wear a mask with Jack. I can be me. At least I think I can. There's a comfort and sense of safety with him, which is interesting, since he's broken my heart twenty times before.

The time between Jack calling me and the time of the party is a blur. Tom calls me and asks me what time he should pick me up to head over to the party. I wonder if Tom will be able to tell I've been talking to someone.

I wonder if he will be able to pick up on my energy and anxiety and excitement.

I finally settle on this black dress and my strappy leopard print heels. I don't like my reflection in the mirror, per usual. Tom arrives at my apartment and he's wearing one of his expensive suits and has a pocket square in his coat pocket. I give myself a final once-over in the mirror, grab my coat, my purse, and the food, and head to Tom's car. In juxtaposition to the whirlwind phone call I just received, the car ride with Tom is tedious, to say the least. Tom asks me about my day and I'm completely distracted by thoughts of Jack. *You don't really want to know about my day*, I think to myself.

We get to the party and my mind is elsewhere. I replay my conversation with Jack in my head and reread our text exchange. After my second cocktail, I get loose lipped and tell Meghan about Jack texting and calling me. She wants to know all about it, and of course, I tell her. I have a huge smile on my face, and then I look across the room at Tom and I wonder if he thinks my smile is for him or someone else. It's almost midnight. I check my phone and I have a missed call from Jack. A twinge of excitement runs through my body once again—I feel like a teenager. Everyone is in the main living room is about to watch the ball drop, so I step outside to return Jack's call. I'm a smoker, so no one will think twice anyway if I'm outside by myself. He answers and I can tell he's partying with his friends—so we laugh and smile and flirt, and he says he'll call this week. I get off the phone and I'm giddy. I step back into the house and rejoin the party as if nothing happened. I stand next to Tom and hold him close, and he kisses me while the ball drops.

My emotional state the next week has shifted. I'm on the same Adderall high, in the same relationship with Tom, have the same amount of work in my career, and my friendships are the same. The only difference this week is Jack. We've been texting all week and we talked for hours on Wednesday night—which is the weeknight that Tom has his kids so it's safe for me to talk with Jack. I feel like I'm walking on clouds. I've officially checked out of my relationship with Tom, although he has no clue. And I feel like I'm able to talk to Jack about anything and everything.

He knows I have a boyfriend, but he also knows that I'm not that into it. Jack lives in San Jose, California, and I live in Kentucky, so it's not like we can just run into each other.

We talk about our moms. I update him on my mom's drinking (she still is), and he tells me that his mom has a drinking problem, too. I feel so seen and understood—a validation Tom is incapable of giving me. I can be open and transparent with Jack. He's a partner at a law firm and practices litigation and family law. He doesn't love the actual work, but he loves the law. Work has been hectic for both of us. Jack casually mentions that he's been using Adderall to keep up with his ever-expanding workload at the law firm. This is my opportunity to be honest about Adderall—I didn't know this was even possible for me. "I take Adderall, too," I say.

Damn it feels liberating to be honest. I'm not going to tell him I have a problem, but I think that since I've mentioned it nonchalantly like he did, then maybe I won't need to hide my addiction from him. Tom will abandon me when he finds out that I'm back on Adderall. We've already been through too much together—this might be the final straw. Maybe Jack will be okay with me taking it? Tom has been through too much with me and Dr. 3, and the tapering of Adderall, and my mood swings going off it. Returning to the drug would be a cardinal sin for Tom—he would never forgive me. But I'm not going off it any time soon. That alone is a good reason to jump the Tom ship and choose Jack. With Jack, I don't have to choose between my relationship and my Adderall—I can have both.

Jack and I brainstorm ways we can see each other, since we live so far away from each other. Then I remember Tom has a conference in San Francisco in February—maybe I can sneak away to meet Jack while Tom is in his conference sessions. Which sounds insane—but it could work. I'm sneaky like that. Only thinking of myself, I'm determined to meet up with Jack. Like any good Adderall addict—when I get an idea in my mind—I make it happen at any cost.

* * *

The trip to San Francisco with Tom starts coming together and I tell Jack when and where I'll be, but I leave out the part about traveling with

Tom. Tom thinks I'm tagging along because I love him, and Jack thinks I'm on a work trip alone. Great.

It's time for Jack and me to meet in the hotel lobby, and I'm in a predicament—the concierge has already seen me with Tom and will now see me with Jack—what will they think and what will they say? I'm not thinking straight. In fact, I'm not thinking at all. I'm just doing what-ever the fuck I want to do without any concern for anyone else's feelings. Which is basically how I am on Adderall—I'm all about me, I'm always in a hurry, and I want to solve things fast—like trying to figure out if I need to be with Jack and flying to San Francisco with my boyfriend under the guise of attending a conference.

I go down to the lobby and there's a message for me at the front desk. There are flowers from Jack that need to be delivered to my room. I can only imagine what they're thinking at this point, and this is the "sane" part of the day. I leave the lobby and head outside to smoke a cigarette to calm down. My heart is beating out of my chest. I'm about to see Jack. He doesn't know I'm here with Tom, and Tom doesn't know I'm meeting up with Jack.

I put my cigarette out in the ashtray next to the doors of the hotel lobby. I take a deep breath. And I see Jack walking along the sidewalk toward me. He's wearing attorney clothes—a suit and a button-up shirt. He looks perfect. We see each other and we hug, and we don't let go. We look into each other's eyes and we can't stop looking at each other. Both of us have smiles on our faces that stretch from ear to ear. "It's good to see you, Jack," I say. "It's good to see you, too, Vitale," he responds. "You look great. You haven't changed a bit."

I'm not hungry because of the butterflies in my stomach and because I'm on Adderall, but I figure I should probably eat something since it's lunchtime. I haven't eaten yet today. We sit down at a table for two—both of us are acting like teenagers in love. I immediately order a bourbon and ginger ale in a short glass. I justify my day drinking with the fact that I'm on vacation, but the truth is I feel so guilty for what I'm doing, I need to numb it with alcohol. Jack orders a whiskey on the rocks. We order food and drinks and we end up talking for hours. We talk about our families, and what we've been doing professionally, and our lives and dreams. And we laugh about the past. We don't talk about Matthew, but we talk about everything else. With Tom, all we talk about is work—it's all we have in common. With Jack, I have everything in common. The combination of Adderall, no food in my stomach, and four bourbons is lethal. The Adderall allows me to drink more because it metabolizes everything in my system so quickly. If I wasn't on Adderall, I'd probably be on the floor passed out by now. Adderall gives me energy and endurance. It also fuels my need for excitement and newness. With Adderall I always want to be awake and "on." There's no place for boring and complacent and normal with Adderall. And secretly meeting up with Jack is anything but boring. Before I know it, I'm completely drunk, and it's 6:30 p.m. and I've missed two calls from Tom. *Shit. What am I going to do?*

"Jack, we need to leave right now," I say in a hurry. I need to call Tom back. I can't hide it anymore from Jack. "I also have something I need to tell you. I'm actually here with Tom." I wait for his response. I don't want to lose him.

"Um, okay," he says. He seems upset by the news, but we're both too drunk to care. I need to meet up with Tom for dinner, but I also need to do something about Jack. He's drunk and can't drive anywhere—and he lives an hour away in San Jose.

I devise an elaborate story to tell Tom. I call him back, and I can tell he's wondering where I am. I confess that I made the last-minute decision to get in touch with Jack since he lives nearby. There is complete silence on the other end of the line following my confession. I look at Jack and I look down at my phone. *What am I doing right now? How in the world do I think this is going to work?* I should probably leave Jack to be with Tom, but I don't want to leave Jack yet. Our connection is electric. "Well, our dinner reservation is in thirty minutes," Tom says, finally breaking the awkward silence. I feel a twinge of remorse. I should have never done this to Tom. *I'm terrible for doing this. What the fuck am I thinking?* Jack looks at me with his big brown eyes, and we lock in a gaze. The chemical rush I experience overrides the remorse.

Then Tom invites Jack to join us for dinner so they can meet. Jack accepts the offer and jokes about meeting my much older boyfriend. Jack

and I walk toward my hotel, and we are completely drunk and not thinking straight. We approach the hotel, and Tom is standing outside on the
sidewalk in front of the lobby doors. I greet him and try to kiss him, but
he steps away. He won't look me in the eyes—hell, I don't want to look him
in the eyes either. I'm afraid if I look him in the eyes, I will be forced to
confront this crazy situation I've created for all of us. I introduce him and
Jack, and they shake hands with force, as if to prove who is more worthy.
We walk to the restaurant and Tom won't hold my hand, choosing to stuff
his hands in his pockets as he interrogates Jack like a son who hasn't made
a good life decision. I'm the one who hasn't made the good life decision.
I'm the reason we are all here. I walk next to Tom to prove my loyalty, and
Jack walks a few feet behind us.

I abstain from alcohol at dinner because I'm hoping I will sober up.
Tom still won't look at me and doesn't engage me in any conversation. This
is all about my current boyfriend sizing up my first love and vice versa. I
finally start sobering up and the weight of what I've done consumes me.
I feel guilt and shame and hatred toward myself. Why can't I just keep
things simple? I created this entire mess. I am justifying my behavior one
minute and then self-loathing the next. It is like a ping-pong game inside
my head: from *You did the right thing, you needed to find out if you still had
feelings for Jack, plus you and Tom hardly have a connection anymore* to *You
selfish bitch, how could you do something so terrible?* I am watching a debate
inside my head—honestly, this would make for quality reality television.
I don't know which side to be on—Tom's or Jack's—I just know I am
stuck between the two. Never did it dawn on me that both of them would
choose *not* to be with me!

We walk back to the hotel in awkward silence. I am remorseful and
shameful, Tom is fuming, and Jack is casually concerned about where he
will be spending the night, since clearly he had assumed we'd be staying
together. To belabor the tormenting encounter, to feed into the drama
more, I agree we stop for a nightcap at the lobby bar, then Jack suggests he
crash in our hotel room.

Tom looks at me with shock and disgust, and I look at Jack and say
no. Tom and I head back to our room. I have no idea what will happen to

Jack—I feel guilty because I got him into this mess. We get to our room and Tom won't speak to me—he takes off his clothes and gets into bed. I am shaking and anxious and overcome with shame as I crawl into bed with him. I can't sleep—I just keep thinking about the day's events and my role in it all and the fact that I had orchestrated all this chaos. Tom quickly falls asleep.

A knock raps on the door. I yell, "Who is it?"

"It's Jack," he yells back through the door. He keeps pounding on the door. Tom calls hotel security because Jack won't leave; he is feeding right into the chaos I created. When I wake up the next morning, Tom is gone. He still has a half-day's conference to attend. I am hung over and weighed down in shame and anxiety and remorse. I get a call from the front desk and it is Jack; he wants to know if he can come up to my room. I am excited to hear from him, but at the same time, I'm shocked that he hung around. I am so hung over, I can barely get up to answer the door. But I do and I immediately lay back down. Jack sits next to me in bed, and we both look at each other and laugh—that's all we can do. Jack says he is uncomfortable sitting on the same bed that I had been sleeping in with my boyfriend, so he asks if we can go downstairs to have breakfast and talk. I can barely function and process what had happened the night before, much less go to breakfast. Fuck. But I agree.

I get up, put on clothes, check my face, take some Adderall and Advil, and head to breakfast. We go to the restaurant downstairs and I'm sure all the hotel staff are wondering what I am doing with the crazy man who was banging on my door the night before. But I am with him, and I am not thinking straight. I allow my feelings and emotions to drive my actions. I allow Adderall to drive my actions. We sit down in a booth, and Jack tells me he wants to be with me and that I need to break up with Tom. I tell him I want to be with him, too, but I need time to sort things out with Tom. Which is partially true—it is true that I need to sort things out with Tom, but it isn't entirely true that I want to be with Jack.

It's time for Jack to drive back to San Jose to work. As he walks toward his car, I feel separation anxiety. I feel alone. Now I'm left to deal with the aftermath. Tom hates me and Jack lives in California. I feel alone and abandoned by my own doing. I walk back to the hotel and get back in bed because I am depressed. Tom texts me to tell me he will be back around lunchtime and that we can walk around the city. It is almost like he is pretending nothing has happened. I agree and text him a bullshit apology, and he doesn't respond. I don't deserve a response. I am selfish. And I hurt someone I love. I get in the shower and my day-old mascara runs down my face as I cry over the loneliness I feel. I feel so lonely and empty inside. It feels like my entire world is over. I feel numb and hollow and alone. This is anything *but* perfect.

Tom arrives back at the hotel and we grab lunch and head down to the pier to walk around. We are both silent, except for small talk. He doesn't want to talk about it—because he never wants to talk about anything— and I don't want to bring it up. I feel emptier than empty, if there is such a thing. I feel hollow and bare and lifeless. Last night's events are replaying in my head repeatedly. It is insane. We walk along the pier when Tom finally starts talking about last night. He starts berating me for my actions and behavior—which I deserve. He tells me how terrible and selfish I am and that my behavior is totally out of line. And I don't disagree with him. I am a terrible person.

He then asks me a question that I am not prepared to answer. "Are you taking Adderall again?" he asks. I don't know how to respond. I can't believe he's asking me this. My hangover, mixed with the Adderall I took this morning and the shame I feel, makes his question unbearable. I started taking it again ten months ago, but I don't want him to know that. Why is he even asking me this? Last night's drama with Jack is a good sign that something isn't right with me. Or maybe it's my weight loss. I had stopped exercising and obsessing over my weight because with Adderall I lose weight without trying.

I keep my Adderall use from Tom because I don't want him to know. But now he's asked me, and I don't know what to say. My silence is all he needs to know my answer. I quickly think about all the possible responses I can give him—I can tell him the whole truth and that I went back on it ten months ago, or I can tell him a half truth and that I went back on it a few months ago, or I can lie and say I am not taking any Adderall. If he searches my purse, he will find the answer—I don't go anywhere without my Adderall. I start calculating my options and how I should respond. I am frightened. If I tell him I am taking Adderall again, he might leave me, and I would be alone and abandoned. If I lie to him, then at least I still have a shot at preserving the relationship, but then I would have to continue to lie. I've already lied enough.

I think about all the damage I caused the night before and I am scared shitless, so I decide to go with the half truth—it is the best way to go. I will admit I am back on Adderall, but I won't admit how long I have been back on it. I've been back on Adderall for nearly a year—and if Tom knows that he would lose it on me. "I'm taking Adderall again," I say without further explanation. I don't know what details to include; I'm so used to lying. I don't look at him because I don't want to see his reaction—I just blurt it out and turn away from him. "Are you serious, Vitale?" he says as if he's surprised. "After everything we've been through—you're taking Adderall again?" I don't know if he's more surprised that I'm taking Adderall again, or by the fact that I am honest about it. He's probably been in denial. But my behavior is so insane that he wants something to blame it on, something to blame for my insanity. He keeps repeating over and over how shocked and disappointed he is. He doesn't know the first thing about Adderall or why I am taking it or why I need it. He doesn't understand the depth of my addiction. Then again, I'm not sure I fully understand. How can he be so surprised? I mean come on—how did he think I'd lost so much weight again without exercising and with the food I am eating? Let's be real. I am back on Adderall—it is the only thing I can count on these days. It is the only thing that makes me feel perfect. It is the only thing that makes me feel safe. "Your behavior last night was so out of character that it had to be Adderall-induced," he declares. I don't respond; I don't want to relive the events of the night before.

He yells at me and belittles me and tells me I'm a liar and a cheater—which was perfect timing given my actions the day before. I am a liar and a cheater. Tom yells at me and I take it. I deserve it. We walk along the pier, and I mentally check out. I am liar. I lied to Tom about Jack. I lied to Tom about the Adderall. And I lied to Jack about Tom. I am in the middle of a storm that I created, and I thrived on it. In some twisted way, I need that storm for survival. I feel the safest in a storm. I feel the safest in the middle of complete chaos.

Tom wants all the answers: why I'm back on Adderall, how long I've been talking to Jack, and why I did this—except I don't know the answers. I just want out of the conversation. It's my fault and I can't change that. We get back to our hotel room, and Tom doesn't say anything else about the Adderall. We go to dinner and have sex as if things are back to normal, but they aren't.

We return to Lexington, and I am overwhelmed with guilt and shame and imperfection. If I were perfect, I never would have allowed this to happen. I never would have been caught. Hell. I never would have gone to San Francisco in the first place. But I'm imperfect, and I can't take it back. *How did I allow this to happen? How could I have done something so terrible? Why couldn't I be honest? Why do I always have to lie?*

* * *

Jack calls me later that week, and he says he wants to fly to Lexington. I'm at a loss. I beg him to wait so I can sort things out with Tom first. I tell him that we don't need to talk until I figure things out with Tom. I do tell him he can write me letters—and he does. I immediately receive two love letters in the mail from Jack, professing his love for me and how our history makes our connection even more meaningful—that we are soul mates. I hang onto every word in those letters. I try to mend things with Tom, but my heart isn't in it. We get back into our regular routine—we eat dinner and drink our martinis and bourbons and go through the motions. We are two shells of people who used to be madly in love with each other. Now we are two people hurting. Hurting badly from our past and have no room to for each other's pain.

It has been three weeks since we got back from San Francisco and I can't shake the memories. Jack grows impatient and he calls me to tell me he has booked a flight to come visit me that week. I panic—how will I handle that with Tom? Who will see us? How will I explain this to Tom? I am living for the chase and I love being pursued—two men are madly in love with me and I am thriving off it. I can't get enough and at the same time, it is too much. Thank God for Adderall, or otherwise I wouldn't be able to focus. I tell Jack I need to think about him visiting—I don't know if it is the best idea. I try to figure out how I will manage being in a relationship with Tom, while also having Jack in town. It is absurd that I even think it is possible to manage. I take a sip of bourbon as I come up with a game plan.

I want to end the relationship with Tom, but I am a coward. Instead, I tell him I need a break—which is total bullshit. Tom asks me for a reason, and I tell him it is because I need time to think about everything—that I need some space. No one ever needs to go on a break. A break is a coward's excuse for a breakup. It's a cheater's excuse to see other people while stringing the other person along. It is sick and I am sick—I am terrified of being abandoned and so I reason that I can get away with all of this. I rationalize it all. I tell myself that if I am on a break with Tom, then it is fine for Jack to come into town—I am not doing anything wrong. Jesus Christ. What the fuck am I thinking?

Jack's ticket is booked, and I get cold feet. I ask him if he can visit another weekend and he says yes. I feel instant relief. Tom and I are on a break, and Jack isn't visiting. Whew. I can breathe. My friends are living for my drama and chaos—it is fun for them to hear about and they don't have to live it. All of this drama is stressing me out. Plus, my next Adderall prescription can't be filled until next week and I don't have enough pills to cover me through the weekend.

That Friday night I go to Meghan's lake house for the night; I need to get away. It is good to be away from the guys and just have some girl time. On the way home from the lake the next day, I get a text from Jack, "I'm at Ramsey's. Come pick me up." It is 8:00 a.m. My heart sinks. What did this text even mean? Is he in town? Holy shit. I call him, and sure enough he is in Lexington. He is forcing himself on me, and I like it. I like not having to make decisions—I want the decisions made for me, that way I am less responsible. That way I don't have to decide. I can put it on someone else. It feels good to have someone pursuing me—to feel attractive—for someone to have flown across the country just for me. Ramsey's is a local diner with a killer breakfast. As soon as I realize he is really in Lexington and I am going to see him, I look at myself in the mirror. I have mascara under my eyes, and I haven't brushed my teeth, and I am wearing yoga pants and an oversized sweatshirt. I am not wearing what I want to wear to see Jack. I want to look hot and sexy and fun, not tired and stressed and comfortable.

I hurry home to change my clothes and clean up my face and take my Adderall. I am almost out of Adderall—how am I going to get through the weekend without it? It's one thing to go without it when it's just me and it's a whole other thing to go without it when I am around another human—and actually be present and focused. Will I be hungry and tired? Will I make it through the weekend? How will I ration out my remaining Adderall? I also need to save a few for work on Monday. All of these thoughts are swirling around in my brain while I am removing my eye makeup. I grab my Adderall bottle from my purse and take two 30 mg XRs—I have only fifteen to get me through until Tuesday and it is Saturday. I normally take seven to nine 30 mg XRs each day. Fuck. How did I let this happen again? How did I let myself run out of Adderall again? Always the same bullshit. I need to refocus—the love of my life decides to fly across the country to see me. And maybe he has some Adderall on him. Anyway, I need to focus. I get dressed and throw my hair into a ponytail. I get in my car and light a cigarette. My nervous system is on overdrive—I'm excited and anxious. Oh yeah—and I have a boyfriend—that I decided to take a break from. What the fuck am I doing? My brain is moving a million miles a minute. I take another puff of my cigarette and my stress level decreases. My body calms down with every inhale of smoke. I throw my cigarette out the window and I text Jack that I will be there in five minutes.

I am used to dating someone twenty-seven years older than me. It feels good to be with someone my own age, someone who knows me, someone who knew Matthew. I pull into the parking lot and unlock the car door. I can't believe this is really happening—this is so exciting. He gets into the car and we just look into each other's eyes. We communicate without words—the amount of sexual energy moving between the two of us is intense. I could feel it coursing through my body. I want to touch him, I want to talk, but I don't know what to say. So I smile and say hello and ask him about his flight. He says he knows he told me he wasn't coming but that was never his plan—he was always coming to see me. I feel worthy. I feel beautiful. I feel wanted. I love how he took control.

Every time Jack and I are in my car stopped at a red light, I look around to make sure Tom isn't in the car next to me. I don't want him to find out. But the places Jack and I are going are not places that Tom and I go to—which isn't saying much because Tom and I have been in hiding for nearly two-and-a-half years. We haven't gone out to restaurants or bars or anything. We just stay in because we've been afraid of someone from work seeing us or someone from his family. Even though the divorce is finalized, we are stuck in our hermit pattern. And we are resentful toward each other. It feels good to be out and dancing and drinking and having fun. And it feels good to be out with someone my own age. It doesn't feel like people are staring and judging us for our age difference. It feels good to be out in the open and free. Tom and I have spent so much time hiding our love and defending it, and less time enjoying it. I don't have to be on guard with Jack—I don't have to be hypervigilant about who might see us or what they might say. We can just enjoy ourselves and not worry about anyone else. It is refreshing.

I decide I will make dinner for Jack and be all homemaker like—I want to come off as this woman who has it all together. I have the career and the friends and the home life, and I want to seem like I can do it all. I want to be able to pull it off. I can be the homemaker and the career powerhouse and be great in bed. I want to be everything—a man's dream. I want to be perfect.

We eat dinner and I am two or three bourbons in and I am getting tired. Normally I would be jacked up on Adderall and I wouldn't be tired, but since I am rationing my Adderall, I don't have much in my system. I am exhausted—emotionally and from running hard in life. Jack says he is tired, too, from the long flight and time change and that he has some Adderall we could take to wake us up. I casually act interested and say yes. If I act too excited, he might be able to tell that I have an Adderall problem. I don't want him to know I am addicted to Adderall, but it is also a relief that I don't have to hide my Adderall from him. It feels like another huge weight is lifted off my shoulders. I can take Adderall and not demonize myself for it. Although Tom isn't breathing down my neck about it, it feels like it. I feel so guilty every time I am around Tom because it is a reminder of my shortcomings. And damn does it feel good to be around Jack and not feel guilty about my Adderall. And it feels good not having to choose between him and Adderall.

We each take two Adderall and wash them down with bourbon. I am ready to go. I hear a honk at the back door and realize my friends have arrived to pick us up. I can't wait for everyone to meet Jack. I feel so proud and worthy and wanted. I am wearing a beautiful black lace Milly dress that I borrowed from a friend. I feel beautiful and sexy and powerful. I have two men after me—Tom and Jack. We go to the bar and take shots and drink liquor and party hard. It feels so good to be out in public.

We get home around 2:30 a.m. and I am in love. I haven't had this much fun in years—maybe since the last time I saw Jack three years ago. We dance in my kitchen to rap music and Van Morrison and we laugh, and we kiss. We can't keep our hands off each other. We make love all night.

We wake up the next morning hung over and love struck. We cuddle and look into each other's eyes and smile. It feels so right. Tom is a distant memory. Jack is what I want—it would make such a good story to say I end up marrying my high school sweetheart and my first kiss—isn't that the stuff movies are made of? And I have it in my bed with me. I get out of bed and hurry to my purse in the kitchen and grab my Adderall bottle and quickly take two 30 mg XRs—I don't want Jack to suspect anything. He is in town for one more night and I feel so lucky. My friends send me tons of text messages saying how much they like Jack and how they have never seen me so happy. It feels right.

* * *

I have to deal with Tom. I need to return his texts; I need to decide my next steps. We work together and we have spent nearly three years together and have been through hell and back. Maybe he is right for me?

Maybe Jack is too aggressive. But maybe I like that about Jack. I want to make the perfect decision, but I don't know what that is.

I walk into Tom's house and I'm practicing what I should say over and over in my head, "I think we should break up. This isn't working anymore." I'm pumping myself up in my head. *You've got this. Stay strong. You're unhappy.* We start talking and I feel remorse for what I've done to him and for being a liar. *What the fuck is wrong with me?* I miss him—which is basically code for I want what I can't have. I don't want Tom to move on—because I'm addicted to being loved. I need to be loved to feel valued. And if I hurt Tom and he moves on, what does that say about me? Does that say I'm not good enough or worthy or beautiful or thin or successful? I don't want him to move on. I want to keep him in my control—because I want to control my own feelings. I don't want to feel abandoned.

I don't have the guts to end the relationship, but I'm overcome with guilt, guilt for Tom and guilt for Jack. I feel pressured from both sides. I need to end this now; I need to get this over with. "I've missed you terribly," he says. "The past few days have given me time to think about us, Vitale. You're the one for me. You're the only woman I'll ever love." He kisses me and I pull away. I need space. "Tom, this isn't working," I say. I can't look him in the eyes. "I think we need to go our separate ways."

* * *

Two months pass—Jack visits me Easter weekend, and now it's my turn to fly to San Jose. Since Jack and I started dating, I've been consumed with thoughts of him and starting a family together. Of this quaint little life, back home in Alabama, where our roots are planted and have reached into our joint hearts. In just eight weeks, we've talked about getting engaged and how we have always been soul mates—ever since we were sixteen. I can't believe someone wants to marry me. I have everything I could have ever asked for—my future husband. Check. A successful career. Check. Amazing friends. Check. A full bottle of Adderall. Check. Everything is finally falling into place. Everything is heading toward perfect.

I fly to San Jose the next morning and I'm excited and nervous and full of disbelief. I can't believe someone wants to spend their life with me. I can't believe Jack chose me. And I'm not sure I even want to be chosen, but the just the act of being chosen is enough for now. I'm wearing a dress that my friends picked out for me—like I needed to be wearing a "I'm almost engaged" dress when Jack picks me up. But I look good and feel confident. I walk to the luggage area to grab my suitcase and Jack is waiting for me with flowers. He's wearing his lawyer suit and I'm wearing my dress and we look good together. I smile at his sweet gesture with the flowers, and at the same time I feel awkward holding the flowers. Like I'm not worthy of getting flowers. He carries my suitcase to the car and we go to his office and I meet his colleagues for the first time. We have mindless conversation and then he signals to me that it's time to leave so we head to his car and then his house—which is this sweet little rental near the ocean. It's within walking distance of a lot of great bars and restaurants.

We arrive at Jack's house and he asks me if I want to go for a walk, and I agree because I want to be agreeable. We walk along this trail that looks over the ocean and Jack suggests we get a picture of the two of us. He sets up the timer on his phone and tells me where to stand. I feel awkward because I hate pictures but go along with it. I'm completely focused on me and how I look, and I just want to be loved. Jack walks over toward me and gets down on one knee and I'm in disbelief. I'm in disbelief that someone wants to marry me. I smile and laugh awkwardly because I don't know what to do—but he proposes, and I say yes and we kiss.

We're in the middle of a forest and I have a ring on my finger, but I feel like a fraud. And the ring feels weird on my hand. I'm excited and I feel safe—Jack chose me. We have the most passionate sex, and we go out to celebrate. Everyone is buying us shots. The time difference and the emotional stress kick in and I take some of Jack's Adderall so I can stay awake and party. That pretty much describes our relationship—one big, drunk party.

The next morning, we wake up as the newly engaged couple. And I fly home the next day. I'm in the airport and I buy a few wedding magazines—*I mean, why not? I'm engaged—I might as well celebrate.* I call my parents and we celebrate. My mom sounds so happy—like she's done her job, her firstborn is engaged. I walk to the gate and my mind is occupied.

I know I need to tell Tom, but if Jack finds out that I called Tom, then I will get in trouble. Jack hates the fact that Tom and I work together. He is always questioning me about whether I have talked to or seen Tom. And the one time I am honest about running into Tom in the elevator at work, Jack completely loses it on me. He wants me to have nothing to do with Tom. I spent three years with Tom, so the least I can do is tell him the news. I don't have to tell Jack that I called him. I pick up my phone and start dialing his number. I had deleted Tom from my phone a few weeks ago as an act of self-empowerment. "If he's not in my phone, then he doesn't mean anything to me."

"Hello," he says, acting like his phone doesn't have caller ID and it's not me on the other end of the line. I play along with his game, "Hey, it's me. Vitale." I don't know how I'm going to tell him. I had rehearsed in my mind what I would say, but it's a completely different story when it's happening. "I have something I need to tell you," I blurt out. I just want to get this over with. "Jack and I got engaged this weekend." Silence on the other end preceded Tom's response, "Wow. Well, congratulations, I guess."

I want to have a conversation with him; I want to go back to normal. But I can't. I'm engaged now—there's no going back. "Best of luck with everything," he says. He hangs up the phone before I can even respond.

At least I can check that off my list. *Tell Tom I got engaged. Check.*

SIX

The Good Wife

My life is moving a million miles a minute—and I haven't thought anything through. *Will I quit my job? When will I move to Alabama? When will we get married? When will I tell my boss? What will people at work think? What are people in general thinking?* I feel completely out of control, and I don't know what I'm doing. *This is what I want, isn't it? I want to marry Jack, right? I just want someone to claim me as their own. I want to be worthy of marriage. I want to be perfect. I spent the last three turbulent years with Tom, and he wasn't going to marry me. And now Jack is. So I should want that, right? I don't even know. But I said yes, so there's no turning back now. Plus, who else would want me? I need to be able to maintain my Adderall and alcohol consumption without judgment.*

Three weeks pass since our engagement and the newness has worn off. I go to see my gynecologist for my annual exam. The doctor comes in and notices the engagement ring on my finger. "Have you thought about when you're going to have children?" she asks. "You're thirty years old; it might be helpful for us to do some routine blood tests to check your fertility." This isn't even on my radar, but I agree. I'm thirty, which is code for "old" in the fertility world. A week passes and I get a call from my doctor with the results. "Vitale, we need to talk," she says. "Your results are serious; your AMH levels are way below the average. I don't know where you are in your timing of having children, but we need to get you to a specialist." This is not what I expect. I don't know if I want to have children, but I may not have the luxury of time to decide. It may be out of my hands.

I get this news on the heels of my sister's wedding—it's in seven days. Bentley is almost two years old now, and Frankie has been seeing her fiancé Clayton for the past seven months. It makes sense that they got engaged—Frankie always needs to be with a man. I don't even know if the ink is dry from her divorce from Bentley's father. My parents hope that Clayton is the answer to their prayers—that Frankie will finally settle down and Bentley will have a stable home. But who knows? I do know that she's not sober—her drug use and lifestyle have calmed down since she started dating Clayton, but I don't know if that's because I don't hear from her as much or if it's because I'm in denial. I'm dreading this bullshit wedding. Who knows how long this relationship will last. Frankie bounces from guy to guy to guy.

The wedding is ridiculous to begin with—the fact that she is getting married seems like a joke in my book. I mean, of course, my sister gets married twice before I get married. I try involving myself in the wedding planning and it is a shit show. I insert myself into the planning of the wedding because I want the control and I am addicted to the chaos with my family and in my own life.

Being at home with my family is never fun with my mom drinking and my sister using drugs, and that is in the back of my mind. My sister's wedding planning stirs up all the chaos at home. I try organizing calls between my sister and my mom to assist with the wedding coordination. My mom would be on the call intoxicated and my sister was fifty-fifty at showing up for the calls. Yet I keep coming back for more. My dad is traveling during the week for his job so he can continue to ignore the chaos. And even though I am six hours away, I am still in the middle of it all.

My life is in complete upheaval. I am no longer with Tom, I am engaged to Jack, I quit the job I love, I am moving back to Alabama, and with my recent fertility news, Jack and I decide to get a jump start on getting pregnant. He wants to go back and work for his family's business, and I follow him like a lost puppy. That's what "good wives" do, right? They follow their husbands; they obey their husbands. I don't recognize myself. I am career driven, ambitious, and successful. Yet, I am willing to give it all up for him.

I pack for my sister's wedding, and I realize that I am almost out of Adderall, and without another prescription, I won't have enough to make it through the weekend. There's no way I can make it through a holiday weekend that includes my sister's wedding without Adderall. I can get the prescription filled by Saturday but that won't help because I will already be in Alabama. I call the pharmacy and ask if I can have the prescription filled earlier for travel purposes. The pharmacist says the best she can do is end of day Friday. I start calculating whether I can pick it up and still make it home in time for the rehearsal dinner. There is no way.

I entertain the idea of missing the rehearsal dinner. *What would I tell my parents, Jack, my sister? What would they think?* I come back to my senses and think of other options—I remember that Meghan is coming down for Frankie's wedding because she is doing her hair and makeup. Maybe she could pick up my prescription for me. How can I position this to Meghan so she won't catch onto my addiction? At this point I am desperate—I need my Adderall and I don't give a fuck what anyone thinks. I call her and try playing it off as just my "Adderall prescription"—no big deal. She agrees to pick it up for me. Thank God.

*   *   *

Jack and I get to Alabama just in time for the rehearsal dinner. It's at my parent's best friend's house and my cousin prepared all the food for it. It is casual and low key. I walk into the house and I can feel the chaos and the tension. My mom has been drinking and everyone is pretending to be happy and excited. People are asking to see my ring and congratulate Jack and me on our engagement—I feel guilty about it—I don't want to overshadow Frankie's weekend. It is her time to shine, not mine. Jack and I drink and party, and I try to be unaffected by my mom's drinking and my sister's wedding drama.

It is Frankie's wedding day—the wedding is at a venue overlooking the mountains, and the reception is at my parents' house. My mom keeps referring to how expensive everything is—in fact, she is already on something and it is only 8:00 a.m. She must have taken some Xanax. Jesus. Today should be all about Frankie, but I am making it all about me. And my mom is making it all about her. We are both not well. Meghan finally arrives, and before even hugging her, I am asking her about my Adderall. She rolls her eyes and gives it to me, and I thank her.

It is two hours until the ceremony, and my mom is nowhere to be found. Meghan is doing Frankie's makeup and all the bridesmaids are hanging out with them while Frankie finishes getting ready. I run upstairs to find my mom—no luck. I look in the garage where I usually find my parents smoking during wintertime—no luck. Okay, she must be outside. I walk outside and my dad is smoking his cigarette in his favorite teak chair right outside the door. "Where's mom?" I ask him in a panic.

"She's out by the back patio table," he says calmly. I'm anything but calm. I rush over to the table, and before I get close to her, I can see her squinty eyes and her mellow posture, and her energy just feels off. Fuck. She's not sober.

"Where have you been?" I ask her. I'm angry. Of course, she's messed up before the ceremony even starts. Why would I expect anything less?

"Well, I tried helping you and Frankie and you clearly don't need my help, so I'm doing my own thing out here," she says. I can tell from her slurred speech and her overly animated hand movements that she is completely out of her mind. She's gone all the way in today. She must be drinking and taking Xanax, a dangerous combination. I can't believe she decided to get this fucked up on Frankie's wedding day. I am filled with so much anger and I don't know what do with it, plus I have Adderall in my system and so I am extra aggressive and intense. I start drinking bourbon to calm my nerves. I am sweating from the two extra 30 mg XR Adderalls I popped after I discovered my mom's absurd behavior.

My family and the rest of the wedding party head to the wedding and that leaves Meghan, Jack, me, and Bentley. I had volunteered to be responsible for Bentley so the others could head to the venue and get ready. Bentley is wearing this sweet tux made for two-year-olds, and it's big on him because he is small for his age. I don't want to be responsible for Bentley because that is a scary idea for me, but I also secretly want to play the role of mom and dad with Jack. I just want to try it on for the day. *What would it be like for us to be parents? To have children?* I don't know if it's possible for me to have kids, but I can pretend right now.

At the reception, my mother's intoxication becomes my focus. Just like when I was a child, her emotions dictate my emotions. She is always so mean and critical when she is drinking—especially with Xanax. I want to control her every move: Who is she going to upset? What will she say? How will she embarrass us today? My dad isn't doing anything about it, so I guess that means I will. I can't focus on anything else. I am ashamed of her drunkenness and I am ashamed of my family. I am overwhelmed with shame. I only care about me and how things affect me. It is all about me. I end up getting blackout drunk at the wedding and go out afterward with my cousins and some of my sister's friends. I get so messed up that I don't even give a toast at the wedding—I almost miss them cutting their wedding cake. I don't want to feel anything, and I make sure of that by drinking more. We get home around 3 a.m. and the only memories I have from that night are from the pictures.

The next morning Jack and I wake up hung over and I realize the damage I have done. "We drank too much last night, Vitale," he says to me as if I don't know. Why does he have to ruin the fun? I don't want to think about how much I drank, I want to get up and nurse my hangover, take some Adderall, and move on with our day. I don't want to think about how rude I was to Frankie—or the fact that I got so drunk I missed making my obligatory toast. I don't want to face the fact that I think her marriage and the wedding are a sham. How long would this relationship last? I'm lying in bed and I get a flashback from Frankie's wedding. Fuck—she and Clayton left their wedding early because of some things my mom said to Frankie. And she was upset with me, too—and rightfully so. While Frankie and Clayton were cutting their wedding cake, I was dancing outside with the entire wedding party—when all of us should have been paying attention to the new couple. I was doing what I wanted to do. I was rebelling. My mom's out-of-control behavior was a domino effect for my behavior, and my dad just sat on the sidelines and watched it all crumble.

"Your dad is going to be pissed at us," Jack says. "I need to talk to him because he's probably questioning me as your fiancé right now. I need to apologize." He is right, but I don't want to focus on it.

"It will be fine," I reassure him. "We don't need to say anything." I am trying to downplay it. My dad saw how much both of us drank and the fact that we went out to the bars until it was practically daylight out.

My dad is standing in the kitchen when I walk in and I can't look him in the eyes; I know he's upset with me. The last time he saw me drink this much was five years ago at a gala, and he sat me down afterward and had a conversation with me about my drinking. My actions the night before are too much for me to confront—I made the entire night about me and the guilt is overbearing. Hell—I don't remember most of the night, which means it got really out of control. I wanted to rush the end of the wedding to go out to the bars. And fuck—I didn't even do a toast to the new couple. In truth—I didn't even plan a speech or buy a dress for the wedding because I wanted to pretend it wasn't happening. But it did happen, and I did everything to numb the reality of it all. My dad knew my drinking was out of control, but I also knew it was unlikely that he would address it—because my family never addresses any problems. But maybe my dad will say something to Jack and me—I mean Jack won't stop talking about it and it is making me anxious.

"Hey, Dad," I say, looking down at the ground.

"Hey there, guys," he says back to Jack and me. I have no idea which direction this conversation is going to go. He has a sad look in his eyes, a deep sadness, which is probably caused by me and my mom. We exchange pleasantries and he doesn't say anything about our drinking. Per usual, we don't address the problem—we just talk around it. My mom is outside smoking and pretends like nothing happened the night before. But I could tell she and my dad are in a fight because he won't even look at her. I look her in the eyes and I can feel the pain and shame between the two of us. She is ashamed of her behavior and I am ashamed of hers and mine.

"Mom, I was out of control last night," I say to her quietly because I don't want anyone to overhear our conversation. I'm not ready to admit that to anyone else yet. I feel that she would be more accepting of my declaration since she was out of control, too.

She looks at me with sober eyes, "I was, too, Vitale." She looks so ashamed and sad.

"It's going to be okay, Mom," I say. "Today is a new day."

For a moment, there is a sense of empathy and understanding between the two of us. I've never had a conversation like this with her, where I am willing to admit my mistake. I normally just blame her. But I can't do that today. Something about the shame and remorse in her eyes makes me want to reach out to her. There is a real and rare and raw honesty between the two of us—for once. *I have more of her inside me than I want to admit.* Her addiction was passed down to me.

I don't want to face my behavior—and quite honestly, I don't remember a lot of it. But the parts I do remember make me cringe: the drinking until three in the morning; the fact that I didn't toast the new couple; I missed the cake cutting ceremony; the fact that the entire day was about me and not my sister. I grab my purse and find my full Adderall bottle and take four 30 mg XRs. I will feel normal again in a few minutes. Thank God. I avoid any real conversation with my dad, but I do apologize. I look at the ground while I am apologizing because I can't look him in the eyes—that would make it all too real.

* * *

Jack, Meghan, and I move on to our next pit stop, which is to look at the house that Jack and I will be living in initially. It is his grandmother's house in Decatur, Alabama. I don't want to live there, but it is temporary, and I want to be agreeable. I don't want to be a difficult and needy fiancé. We pull up to the ranch style house, and it is in a 1990s neighborhood. I am still hung over and full of guilt, but Meghan is with us so she can also give her opinion on the living arrangements—I need my best friend's opinion for this major life decision.

We walk into Nana's house and it is fully furnished in 1970s décor. There is a peacock on the wall of the second living room, and the couch is striped with dark brown and light brown alternating. I look miserable, but I have done harder things before. I can do this right? And it won't be forever. Meghan looks me in the eyes and tells me it will be okay. She can tell I am totally shocked by the reality of it all—standing in Nana's house it finally hits me. I am soon going to be living in this house with Jack. I feel scared and alone and uncertain. But there is no turning back now. I have already quit my job. I have already found someone to take over my lease in Lexington. The deal is done. I have to follow through.

We leave Nana's house and the three of us head to the lake to meet up with Jack's friend and some of our old friends from high school. In fact, I haven't seen a lot of them since high school. We go out on the lake and I drink too much, too fast, on a stomach that is empty and on Adderall. Meghan and I drink like we are teenagers away from our parents. She handles it better than I do. I end up acting ridiculous and passing out before dinner time. I'm sure I made a great first impression with his friends. I wake up in bed, alone, at 5:00 a.m. the next day. I am hung over and ashamed. I can't remember what I did or said the night before, but I remember being out of control. I remember pissing off the girlfriends and wives of Jack's friends. Great. I get out of bed in a haze and I go looking for Jack. I go outside and find him buck naked in the backyard, and he is still drinking with one of his friends. Holy fuck—it is 5:00 a.m. and he is still partying. I call for him and he ignores me. I feel hurt and scared. I know this isn't good, but I feel trapped.

I go into the room where Meghan was sleeping, and she is packing up her stuff. I tell her what Jack is up to and her eyes get big. She looks concerned. I can't take on her concern because that would make it all too real. I won't be able to handle it. She needs to get back on the road to Lexington, but I feel so alone, and I don't want her to leave. Since I am still so hung over, I ask her to drive me to the nearest gas station before she heads out. I need caffeine and food. We get in her car and start driving and she stops in the middle of the street. "Vitale, are you sure you want to do this?" she asks. "Are you sure you want to marry someone who drinks and parties this much? You can always change your mind." She is right, but her concern is too much for me. I make some excuse for Jack. "He doesn't usually act like this," I respond. But deep down I know this is his normal behavior. I know I am lying to myself, and so does Meghan. We both know I am heading down a dark road. If I admit it out loud, it will be real, and I won't be able to hide from it anymore. So, I lie and pretend everything is okay. I assure Meghan that I am making the right decision. She knows I am scared, so she drops it. I will have to learn this one on my own.

I get back to the house and Jack has passed out on the bed. It is now 6 a.m.—he has a flight back to California leaving at 1 p.m. and I want to go ahead and get on the road to Kentucky, but I don't want to leave him. If I leave without telling him he will get pissed, and I don't want to deal with that. Plus, I don't want him to blame me for missing his flight. And that would happen. I sit in the backyard, all alone, waiting for Jack to wake up. I am sad and scared and lonely. I don't know what to do—I feel so helpless. I take some more Adderall to try to feel better, but it just makes things worse. I am obsessing about Jack and our future and questioning my decision. Around noon, I am finally able to wake Jack. I tell him what time it is and that he is going to miss his flight. He jumps out of bed and goes to take a shower. I start packing his things—and he walks into the room and puts his arms around me, and we embrace. For a few minutes I feel less alone. Since he is going to miss his flight, he decides to ride back with me to Lexington and catch a flight out of Lexington the next day.

We get on the road to Lexington, and we listen to music and talk about our move and our life together. We romanticize it all because the reality of it is too much. If either of us pause for a second to really think about what we are doing, we won't be able to handle it. One of us would probably jump out of the moving car. So we pretend. We pretend everything is okay. I don't smoke the entire ride back, which is difficult, but I want to prove to Jack that I can quit. He wants me to quit smoking. We both agree our partying days are over, and we need to get serious about my fertility and having a baby. The conversation on the drive home goes from light and fun to heavy and real. The reality of it all is hitting me. I am engaged and moving to Decatur, Alabama. Decatur is a small town thirty minutes outside my hometown, and I have no community there. I don't know anyone, except for Jack and his family and it's basically a shithole. The nicest restaurant is the new Mellow Mushroom—what am I doing? My friends are completely shocked that I'm moving there. I'm shocked, too. I change the music on my iPod to distract me from my thoughts.

We get back to my place around 9:00 p.m. and I go straight to the kitchen and pour myself a drink. I need something to take the edge off my reality. I need to focus on nothing. I don't want to think about my infertility, or my behavior at my sister's wedding, or Jack's drinking or anything. I just want to calm down. I don't want to think about anything. Jack notices that I am drinking, and he loses it. He can't believe I am drinking after the conversation we had in the car. He says he didn't realize I drank as much I do—that I must have a problem. And that I only care about myself. I feel bad enough about myself; I don't need his help. Thanks, though. And I really don't think he has much room to talk, seeing that he stayed up drinking until 5:00 a.m. I apologize to him and pour my drink out—I want to prove to him that I don't have a problem. I want him to think I am normal. I want him to love me. I don't want to be abandoned.

He flies home the next day and I feel empty. I am consumed with guilt and shame from the events of the past week and how much I drank and about my infertility and Jack. I feel so lost and broken. I don't feel safe. I don't know what I want. I don't know where to turn. But I do have my Adderall—at least I have that. I have a full bottle and that's the little bit of safety I need right now. I need something to distract me from my reality. I take five 30 mg XRs with water and go outside to smoke. I need a release. Jack is pressuring me to move to Alabama the weekend of July Fourth, which is only five weeks away. I feel pressured that the move is too soon. He wants me away from Tom. I am not allowed to speak to Tom or to be around him, and now he needs me to move. My gut tells me the move is too soon, but I have so much going on in my head that I can't separate my real thoughts from my fake thoughts. I don't know if I am justified in my thinking, or if I need to compromise more and move when Jack wants me to move. I question everything I am doing—I don't know it, but I can't trust myself. My life is moving a million miles an hour and I can't stop it. I can't stop the merry-go-round to hop off.

I can't shake the nagging mix between feeling like a failure of a woman because I don't know if I am ready to get pregnant, and then also a failure at standing up for what I really want for myself—which is to stay in Lexington. I don't want to move. And I don't want to move to Alabama or be engaged—but I don't want to say it out loud. I am engaged and that means I need to follow through on my commitments—something I am not too good at doing with men in the past. I want to rewrite my relationship pattern—I said yes when he proposed so that means I need to hang in there. Even my mother advises me to go along and "be the dutiful wife," but she doesn't know that being his dutiful wife means putting up with a man who wants to control me.

We are in my kitchen and he starts accusing me of drinking and smoking too much—he says I am not taking my fertility seriously. I still haven't quit smoking and I am still drinking a lot—so he is right—but honestly there is so much change going on in my life, what does he expect? And he doesn't even know about the Adderall. I am so tired of his controlling bullshit—telling me where I can go, who to talk to, what not to drink, and keeping tabs on my vices—that I agree to all of it just to make him happy. I can't handle his tight grip anymore. In bed Jack asks me to give him a blow job. I tell him I don't want to because I am not in the mood and I am exhausted. And that is the truth. Jack doesn't like me saying no, so he starts yelling, "You never give me head, which makes you pretty worthless as a fiancé."

Then, he pushes my head down and holds me there and forces me to give him a blow job. It is the lowest I've ever felt. I'm having an out of body experience—my jaw is tight and every muscle in my body is tense. I don't know whether to continue or stop. Tears start falling from my eyes, and I force them to stop—crying will only make it worse. I can't believe I'm engaged to someone who is forcing me to do this. It is this moment that I know I am doing the wrong thing. I can't hide from it anymore. This is too fucked up to hide from. I am in complete shock. How the fuck did I get myself into this situation? How did I allow myself to be treated so disrespectfully? And how did I not know he was like this?

I walk back into the bedroom and his eyes are closed—he is pretending to be asleep. It is total bullshit. I was just forced to do something I didn't want to do by my fiancé—by the man I am going to spend my life with. The reality of what just transpired is too much for me, so I climb into bed with him and try to go to sleep. Our backs are facing each other—I feel stuck. I feel stuck in a relationship with a very controlling man—with a man I thought I knew but don't know. It is fucked up. But I don't know how to get out.

* * *

At work, I scroll through my email and notice one from a recruiter on LinkedIn. I typically dismiss these emails—but this one seems too good to be true—it is a recruiter wondering if I would be interested in applying for my same position but at a law firm in Birmingham, Alabama. They don't even know I am moving to Alabama, but the timing is perfect. It is something I could look forward to—have a law firm marketing job at another law firm. The timing is uncanny. I will have to keep this one to myself for now—but it is a glimpse of light in a very dark tunnel.

It is 2:00 a.m. and I am in the middle of my living room putting together more boxes for the move. I have been going nonstop since I got home from work at 6:00 p.m. It is too much. I am on my fourth bourbon; I have smoked half a pack of cigarettes, and have taken a few extra Adderall. I am a mess. I come across a box of love notes that Tom has written me over the years. I sit down in the middle of the living room and begin reading them. I am on the third love letter when I lose it. I start full body crying—tears so thick and heavy that I can't see out of my eyes—tears so fierce and fast that I can't stop. I am half drunk and finally realizing the weight of my world. My whole body is convulsing from sadness and aloneness. The reality of it all finally hits me. And I am consumed with tears and sadness and truth. I can't avoid the truth any longer.

Here are my truths: I am engaged to a man who I thought I knew but I don't; I am leaving a career that I don't want to leave; I am moving to a place I never wanted to live; I miss Tom; I struggle with infertility; I don't want to stop drinking or smoking; I am addicted to Adderall; I am confused; I am alone and afraid; and I don't want to tell my friends that I am having second thoughts because I can never take it back; and I can't trust my decisions. I don't recognize myself or my choices. I don't know who I've become. I don't know what I want, or what that even looks like. I feel so imperfect.

I pick myself up from the living room floor and stumble to my bedroom carrying my bourbon and the love notes from Tom. I climb into bed and cry myself to sleep. I am the most afraid I've ever been. I have no idea about the direction of my life or what I am doing. I get out my phone and start to text Tom, and then erase the message.

It is two days before my big move and Jack and his cousin are in town helping me pack. I make sure all the bourbon and cigarettes are nowhere in sight—if Jack finds any evidence of my drinking and smoking, he'll completely flip out on me, and I don't want to deal with that. So I lie. It is easier. My friends planned a farewell dinner for me, and it is time to get ready. My apartment is a total wreck—there are boxes everywhere and I don't know where my bras and panties are or my hairspray or hair straightener. I didn't think about needing this stuff before I packed it. I am not thinking clearly.

Jack and his cousin are moving boxes to his truck, and I hop in the shower. The hot water streams down my face and I just stand in the shower motionless. Five minutes pass and I wake up out of my daze. I get out of the shower and wrap a towel around my hair and body. I forgot to bring my clothes into the bathroom to change into, so I walk across the living room in my towel looking for my bra and underwear and an outfit. I don't even think about Jack's cousin being in my apartment, and the fact that I am walking around in a towel in front of him. It hasn't even occurred to me that what I am doing is wrong.

"Did you really just walk in front of my cousin in just your towel?" Jack says. "What are you thinking? I can't believe you'd do that. You're such a slut." I am in disbelief—I can't believe my fiancé called me that. And I am moving tomorrow—for him. Fuck. All I've been doing is whatever the fuck he wants me to do. I wouldn't be walking around in my towel in front of his cousin if I didn't have to move tomorrow. Jack is the one who wants me to move to Alabama so quickly. He is the one making all the demands and calling all the shots. And I am letting him. I let him. And now he is calling me a slut. "And you cuss too much, and it's unladylike," he says, picking me apart.

It is time to meet my friends at the restaurant, and I'm trying to hold it together. I have a few drinks to numb the pain. I feel trapped. The Jack I knew before we got engaged is not the Jack I know now—it is like Jekyll and Hyde. He was a great man before our engagement and became a sociopath after our engagement.

My farewell dinner is bittersweet. It is wonderful being surrounded by all my closest friends and it feels good that they want to celebrate me. But we all know I am making the wrong decision. We all know it, but we are all too afraid to say it. I think everyone is in shock. Jack and I are walking toward my car, and Meghan stops Jack. "You better take good care of Vitale," she tells him. He, of course, assures he that he will. I laugh to myself—of course he'll take care of his "slut" fiancé. There's nothing I can do right. Every step I take is criticized. I want to interject and tell Meghan to save me—that Jack is controlling and crazy and he isn't going to take good care of me. But I am too scared.

We get back to my apartment and we climb into bed. We both have a slight buzz—which is interesting—Jack gave me permission to drink tonight. I don't know the rules of the game. Jack makes them up and I don't know how to play them. One day he will be fine with me drinking and the next day he won't. So it is easier for me to lie or just not drink. But not tonight—it is my last night in Lexington. I am too sad to not drink. I am too emotional. We lay in bed and start having drunk sex—it is passionate and angry and sad. Jack is being aggressive and part of me likes it. We finish having sex—he is able to orgasm, but I am not—I am too disconnected from him and the relationship.

We lay in the bed and have a superficial conversation and talk logistics for the move tomorrow. "How many people have you slept with, Vitale?" he asks out of nowhere. The question completely catches me off guard. I have slept with sixteen people, but I don't know how he will handle that number. I quickly start considering my options—I could tell him my real number, or I could give him a fake number, or I could not respond. I feel so much pressure—my fiancé called me a slut just a few hours before this. I don't know how to handle his question or how to respond. I decide to lie. I don't want to deal with his judgment. I lie and tell him I have slept with ten people. That seems realistic. I am thirty years old and I was eighteen when I lost my virginity. Ten people seems totally normal. And in fact, sixteen people is totally normal. Jack looks relieved when I tell him that number, like he expected it to be five or ten times as much. I don't know why it even matters. His relief gives me relief. I feel like I can breathe—at least for a little while. I lay down on the bed and turn my back toward him—I can't face him right now.

We wake up early the next morning—it is time to move. I grab my Adderall bottle and take five 30 mg XRs—it is more than my normal morning dose—but there is so much to get done. I don't have any time to waste.

* * *

We arrive at Nana's house and it is dusk. Jack's mom meets us there— she is our welcome committee—at least with her I feel safe. Her presence makes me feel calm. And I need calm amid such intense chaos, anything to keep me calm.

The first week in Decatur isn't too bad. Jack and I play house and it's fun. He goes to work at his family's lumber mill at 5:00 a.m. and I get up with him and make him breakfast. *Who the hell have I become?* I never make myself breakfast, much less for a man. I am turning into a regular house-wife. As soon as he pulls out of the driveway, I take my daily Adderall and go outside and smoke three or four cigarettes. I hide the cigarette butts so Jack won't find them. I am living a lie, and the lies keep piling on and getting bigger and bigger.

I need nicotine—plus I am jacked up on Adderall. And Adderall with-out smoking is like drinking my bourbon without ginger ale—I never do it. I am taking five 30 mg XRs in the morning, and three to four more in the afternoon, depending on my mood and task list and need for numbing. Jack is working all the time. He wakes up at 5:00 a.m. to go to work and then comes home at around 6:00 p.m. I could be a stripper during the day, and he wouldn't know it. I can take as much Adderall as I want and get away with it. It is the only normal thing I can cling to in my life.

During the day I keep myself busy with productive procrastination. I am working remotely for my law firm for the next five weeks, so that keeps me busy. Otherwise I'm doing laundry, figuring out wedding details or meal planning. I basically stay in the Adderall zone all day to keep my mind off my life. Jack gets home from work around 6:00 p.m. and I have dinner waiting for him. We are living a life that I never wanted. I want to work and have a life and career and friends and be social. I don't want to wait around all day for my husband to come home. That isn't in my DNA. But I play the part well. I can lie with the best of them.

Our first week living together is our best—we make love like we are in love—or maybe it is more aggression. Maybe we are taking our hate out on each other. Either way—it's passionate. And it feels like it's what we are supposed to be doing as a newly engaged couple living together. For a week, the weight of my reality is lifted. For a week, I am able to play homemaker and pretend everything is okay.

It is time to find a doctor in Alabama to prescribe me Adderall. Dr. 7 in Kentucky says he will still be able to prescribe for me, but I want more Adderall and I don't want to worry about running out. And it will be easier to get Adderall in Alabama than it is in Kentucky. The regulators in Kentucky have cracked down on doctors prescribing this class of drugs, and so most doctors have stopped prescribing it. And there is no way I can fill multiple prescriptions—my days of doctor shopping and pharmacy shopping were over in Kentucky. But in Alabama that isn't the case. They are behind the times. Alabama's regulations haven't caught up with Kentucky's. I google doctors and call around until I find a doctor with an appointment available in the next few days. Thank God. I don't want to run out of Adderall with everything else going on. Adderall keeps me perfect. I can stay thin and beautiful. In the middle of everything going on, I need to be thin and perfect.

The day of my appointment, I tell Jack I am going to Huntsville to visit with my parents. This is bullshit, since I am only going there for Adderall. I pull in the parking garage of Dr. 8's office and look at the directional signage to find his floor and suite number. I am excited and anxious. I am excited over the possibility of another Adderall prescription, and I am anxious over the possibility of being identified as a drug seeker and being turned down.

I sit in the reception area for twenty minutes until my name is called. I get up—but not too eagerly—and follow the nurse back to Dr. 8's office. I walk in and sit down in his upholstered chairs. He asks me the standard questions—it is like old times—and I answer them all perfectly. He is one of those doctors that postdates prescriptions, so he gave me three at once—one for this month, one for the next month, and one for the following month. I have hit the doctor jackpot—I am leaving with three prescriptions. Fuck yes. I leave his office and celebrate in the elevator. I am back in business.

My Adderall consumption goes from five 30 mg XRs a day to seven or eight 30 mg XRs a day. I take more because I can, and the more I take, the more I can get done, and the more I stay distracted from my reality.

In the back of my mind I don't think Jack and I are going to make it. Too much has happened—too much hurt. I continue the interview process with the law firm in Birmingham—I want to have a backup plan. I need to have something else to look forward to. They want to hire me, but they need me to live in Birmingham—making the commute from Decatur isn't good enough. Maybe if this doesn't work out, I can move to Birmingham? We'll see.

SEVEN

Disaster in Decatur

I survive my first week living in Decatur, and it is time for the weekend. Jack's family is having a huge Fourth of July party, and his extended family will be there. We get to the party and I feel totally out of place. Jack pays no attention to me—he is avoiding me but pretending that everything is okay in front of his family. But it isn't. We made it through the week, but he can't fake it anymore. He gets really drunk, and I pretend that I no longer drink bourbon, so I drink beer. I pretend that I am a good girl with no past and no previous sex partners. I pretend to be the perfect girl.

Everyone is drinking heavily at the party. In fact, I am the most sober, which is a first. The party goes on all night and I am miserable. I feel out of place and abandoned and unloved and unworthy. Jack ends up leaving the party to drive four wheelers with his cousins. He leaves without telling me and I have no idea how long he will be gone.

An hour passes and there is still no word from him, and so I decide to go to sleep in his sisters' room. I feel totally out of place and keep falling in and out of sleep. There are loud noises in the room next door that wake me up—and it is Jack. I slowly get out of his sister's bed and walk next door. I find him climbing in bed in his childhood bedroom—he is beyond drunk. I want him to love me, so I lay down next to him in his bed. He looks repulsed by me. I put my hand on his back and he moves away from me. I don't know what I have done to make him so distant and angry. "You are a slut and a liar," he exclaims. "There's no way you only slept with ten people. You've probably slept with ten times that. I can't believe anything that comes out of your mouth." I can't believe he is holding this against me. Why are we even still talking about this bullshit? I am tired of lying—about Adderall, about smoking, about drinking, about the number of people I've slept with. I am tired of this conversation. "Fine; I've slept with sixteen people," I blurt out. He looks shocked and moves farther away from me. He calls me a slut and a liar and tells me again that he can't believe anything that comes out of my mouth. I feel like a terrible person. I feel dirty and unwanted and unlovable. My own fiancé doesn't even want to be near me. I am damaged goods. I am completely damaged.

The next morning, I wake up and head back to the house without Jack. He is still sleeping and hung over. And I don't want to be around him right now anyway given the conversation we had the night before. My fiancé thinks I am a lying slut. I go back to the house and cry—I don't know who to tell or what to say or how to feel. I just feel so damn alone. I am living in Decatur, Alabama, without any support. I haven't told anyone how bad things are or how controlling Jack is—I can't deal with the judgment. I have allowed myself to become a victim—I don't recognize myself anymore.

Since my law firm let me work remotely to transition out of my job, I also agreed to make a few visits back to Lexington to work onsite. This is mostly for selfish reasons—I can still pretend I live in Lexington and that nothing has changed. Even if it is only for a few days it is better than nothing. It is better than the heaviness of my life in Decatur. It is time to leave for my first trip back to Lexington and Jack is pissed. He doesn't trust me and doesn't like the fact that I will be in the same city as Tom. He is jealous and possessive. I haven't talked to Tom since I told him I was engaged. When we pass each other in the office, I act like I don't know him. What I have done to our relationship is too much to bear. To avoid him means I can avoid thinking about it. Plus, if I talk to him, I will be chastised by Jack. And I can't handle any more of that. I pack my things and make sure I have my Adderall with me—I wouldn't want to spend a week in Lexington without it.

I am working out of the Louisville office, and so is Tom. I feel this pull to stop by his office and tell him how sorry I am. I am lonely and disconnected from Jack; I need something familiar. I need to look Tom in the eyes so he can see how trapped I am. We were together for three years and he knew me. He knew my soul. I also want to be near someone who doesn't hate me or call me a slut, someone who loves me as I am—flaws and all. Someone who doesn't care how many people I have slept with. Someone I feel safe with. And right now, that feels like Tom. I feel so empty and so alone that it is all I can do to keep myself from walking into his office. I go back and forth in my head—because I know that Tom and I never officially ended our relationship, and to initiate a conversation with him could be dangerous. But I am miserable with Jack and Jack doesn't even love me. He despises me. And I am engaged to him. I can't handle it anymore. I go to the restroom to check my outfit and my makeup—I want to make sure I look good. I leave the restroom and walk toward Tom's office.

I stand in the middle of the doorway of his office. He senses someone is at his door, so he looks up and it is as if he has seen a ghost. We look into each other's eyes and we don't even have to speak. I can feel the sorrow and hurt in his eyes. I look down at the floor and take a deep breath. I have no idea what to say. I look back at Tom. "I just wanted to tell you how sorry I am for hurting you," I say. I don't skip a beat. I don't tell him how bad things are because I don't want him to know. Then he would be right. He thinks Jack is crazy and he is right. I am lonely and want excitement and affection and chaos and so I move toward it. I move toward the chaos.

Tom says he misses me and asks if I am okay. He is the first person who has asked me that—maybe he is the only person who is willing to deal with the answer. My friends want to ask, but they are too scared. And I haven't revealed all the insanity to them anyway. Tom doesn't know everything that is going on, but he knows me. He can tell there is a deep sadness and unsettledness inside me. I feel seen and heard for the first time in months. We don't have much privacy to talk in his office—and if anyone had seen us, they would have wondered what was going on between us. The news of us dating had rocked the office politics and then I got engaged to someone else and moved. Trust me—I have made quite the statement. I can only imagine what people will think if we start up again. Tom knows I am in pain and he offers to have me over at his new house that night so we can talk. I tell him I will have to think about it. He texts me his new address, and I reply that I will see him around 7:00 p.m. I want to say yes, but I know where that will go. It would only lead to bad things—to more chaos. But I also feel safe with Tom—or safer than I feel with Jack.

I am staying at Meghan's house while I am in Lexington, and I tell her that I have a work function to attend that night. I don't want her wondering where I am, and I sure as hell don't need her knowing I am going to see Tom. She would know exactly where that is leading.

Tom has bought a new house and I am happy for him. It feels like a fresh start—for both of us. I pull into his gravel driveway and walk to his front door. I am nervous and anxious—but I also feel comfortable and familiar. At least I know what I get with Tom. Jack is a ticking time bomb, and I have no idea what mood he will be in from time to time. Tom opens the door and we lock eyes and embrace. He holds me and I hold him, and tears stream down my face. I don't know where to turn. Tom gives me a tour of his house and I am so happy for him. We go into his kitchen and he makes himself a drink. He offers me a drink, but I decline, saying that I am trying to cut back—when in reality, I don't want Jack to find out.

I confess to Tom everything that is going on, and he is speechless. And at the same time, he knows that Jack is insane. How could he see it and I couldn't? Tom walks toward me, and he holds me. He puts his face close to mine and he tries to kiss me. It is too much. I push him away and tell him I can't right now. I am engaged and it is complicated, and this will complicate things even more. I feel guilty for leading him on. For making him think it is okay to try to kiss me. I grab my things and tell him I need space to think and I leave. As I am driving home, I realize I had restarted the love triangle. I had reopened the door to Tom and me.

* * *

I get back to Decatur later that week, and it's as if Jack knows that I have seen Tom. Like he has some sixth sense, or maybe he can feel my guilt. I am anxious and tense and afraid of him. If past behavior is a predictor for future behavior, then I am fucked—on all fronts. I am fucked in terms of how Jack will treat me, I am fucked in terms of having an affair with Tom, I am fucked in terms of blowing shit up and creating chaos.

Jack and I lay in bed together with his back turned toward me. I can feel the distance between us. Our relationship is broken beyond repair. I put my hand on his back and ask him about his week and how he is doing. He acts like he is completely inconvenienced by the mundane chitchat. He turns around and I can see anger in his eyes. "You are an untrustworthy slut," he says. "You're a cum dumpster." I am dumbfounded. My fiancé just called me something that no woman should ever be called. I look at him with so much pain and hurt in my eyes and I turn away from him. He feels righteous and keeps going on and on about my promiscuity and lying. He's finally finished and turns away from me. My body is paralyzed. I don't know what do to or even what has just happened. And to some degree, I feel like I deserve it. I initially lied to him about my number of partners. And I feel guilty about seeing Tom the day before. I have turned into someone else, someone who allows a man to call her unthinkable things—someone who has turned her life upside down for a controlling man, someone who is acting like a victim.

The next morning, I replay our conversation over and over in my mind. I don't even want to say the words out loud. I don't want to admit what he has called me. I have changed my life for a man who could call a woman a cum dumpster. You've got to be fucking kidding me. What the fuck am I doing? I need to get out, but I don't know what to do. I feel stuck. Maybe I deserve to be called that? Maybe this is just a phase he is going through? Maybe he will change?

What would people think if they knew how Jack is treating me? What would that mean for my future? I know in my bones that our relationship isn't going to work, but I am not ready to admit it. I am not ready to face it. I am so scared of being abandoned that I am willing to be treated terribly. Anything to avoid being alone and abandoned.

I am sneaking alcohol and cigarettes because Jack doesn't approve of them. Being forced to quit something never works—you have to want it for yourself. I go to run a few errands on Saturday and I smoke a few cigarettes while I am away from the house. I keep perfume in my car for just this reason—and I spray it on me before I go back to the house. Jack is there when I get back—he asks me if I have been smoking. I am sick of lying. "Yes, I smoked two cigarettes," I confess. "I could be marrying a woman with perfectly good ovaries," he snaps back.

The next several weeks there is nothing I can do right. Jack goes out of town the next three weekends and leaves me at home by myself. He totally ignores me. He never calls me while he is away, and I am left to worry. I don't even know where he is most of the time. How did I end up in this? And during the week, we are ships passing in the night. He comes home late enough to avoid me. And when he can't avoid me, he plays nice. He acts as if everything is fine. He acts like it never happened. We fake it as much as we can. My Adderall intake is increasing—I am now up to eight 30 mg XRs during the day and two more in the afternoon. I am trying to balance transitioning things with my current job, planning a wedding that I know isn't going to happen, applying for the new job in Birmingham, and dealing with my roller coaster of emotions. I am jacked up 24/7 because it keeps me distracted. I sneak cigarettes and drink beer and hide it all from everyone.

And then there's my family. My parents are keeping Bentley a lot, which means my sister and her husband are doing drugs and back to their usual behavior. When I was in Lexington, I could shield myself from the family drama, but I am in Alabama now and live thirty minutes away from my parent's house—and it isn't as easy to escape the family drama. My parents expect me to visit them and watch Bentley. On top of everything else going on in my life, I am expected to be the perfect daughter. And what's even worse is that my parents never once ask to visit me or check on me. I am struggling all alone in Decatur and they can't even visit. But I am expected to visit them. I call my mom because I am lonely and looking for advice and the entire call turns into a lecture of how I am supposed to watch my nephew now that I live in Alabama. Seriously, I can hardly keep it together, much less watch my nephew—and it isn't my fucking responsibility. I am in pain, and all my parents care about is themselves and how I can help them.

"Vitale, you've been in Decatur for three weeks and you still haven't come to help me with Bentley," my mom says. "I can't do this alone and you need to help me like you're supposed to. All you're doing is thinking about yourself and doing your own thing."

I don't know how to respond. I'm in pain and she wants me to help. Her speech is slurred and she's being critical, so I know she's intoxicated. But I feel guilty—maybe I need to be helping, maybe I am selfish and only thinking about myself?

"Okay, Mom, I will come get Bentley—what day this week works for you?" I say hesitantly. "Tomorrow would be great because I need to work," she responds. Tomorrow comes and I get in my car to drive to my parents' house. I don't know the first thing about kids. How am I going to entertain Bentley all day? I don't even know what kind of food he eats or if he still wears diapers. He is just two years old, but I don't know what that means in terms of his development. I walk into my parents' house and my mom hands him to me. She doesn't even acknowledge me or thank me for helping. She's not sober—at least Bentley won't have to be around her all day. I've taken five 30 mg XRs, so I'm in Adderall mode. Give me the kid and let's get today done. Let me check this off my list so they will lay off me.

I'm angry and resentful all morning, and it wears off as soon as I take Bentley to the park. I figure we can feed the ducks like when I was a kid. Bentley is so sweet and innocent; he calls me "Aunt Lolly" because he can't pronounce my name. Today is the first time in two years that I've spent an entire day with him. I've been avoiding him and the pain and the family drama, but I can't escape it today. I can't escape how similar we are—we are both broken. I'm broken from Jack and my mom, and Bentley is broken from Frankie. We both feel unsafe and don't know what the future holds for each of us. Our souls are similar—sometimes too similar. The entire day is really sweet, but I also want it to end. I'm not good with kids and hanging out with him is just a reminder of my own infertility. I'm good at working and Frankie is good at making babies—we can't have it all. It's getting close to the evening and it's time for me to take Bentley back home to my parent's house. At least I could help today. At least now I'm not the terrible aunt who never spends time with her nephew.

My mom drinks or takes Xanax, or both, most of the time now. In fact, it is a rare occasion when I catch her sober. And on top of everything else going on—I want a mother so desperately. A mother who senses I am in pain and makes it all go away. A mother who knows I am in trouble and supports me in finding a way out. A mother who cares enough to drive to Decatur to take me out to lunch and listen to *me*. I am far away from my friends, my fiancé is avoiding me, my parents won't visit me—I feel so alone and abandoned.

There is chaos all around me, and the common denominator is me. Tom is texting me daily—and I ask him to stop because I don't want Jack to find out. I create a new Gmail account and tell him he can only contact me there. I am sneaking around and feeling guilty for it. I haven't kissed Tom, so I justify my behavior. Jack isn't meeting my needs, so I have an excuse. I am throwing more kerosene on the fire. And it could blow up at any minute. It's almost like nothing has changed—I am still on Adderall, and I am addicted to the chaos and drama once again.

* * *

My final work trip to Lexington arrives—it will be the last time in my office and my final few days as a Lexington resident. I don't want to let go. My new reality is too much to bear. I feel so lonely and afraid—I don't know where to turn. I call Tom against my better judgment—I want to be wanted. I go over there for drinks and conversation. I don't tell him about Jack because I don't want him to know how bad things are. They are bad. When the man you're about to marry calls you a slut with bad ovaries, it's pretty bad. Tom and I talk and talk, and I romanticize our time together. We have a long and twisted history. Tom walks over to me and he leans in to kiss me and I don't stop him this time—I want to feel his touch. He wants me to stay the night and I agree—I am in a trance. I can't help myself. I end up sleeping with Tom. I just want to be wanted and needed. I don't want to be abandoned. I don't want to be alone. I've been unfaithful once again—what is wrong with me? Why can't I call things off with Jack and then decide if I want to jump back in with Tom? I'm too scared. I leave

Tom's house full of shame. I don't even recognize myself anymore. I keep repeating the same patterns over and over.

I make the drive back to Decatur and you can read the shame all over my face. Jack will know something happened. I don't call him, and he is texting me nonstop asking where I am and why I am not answering my phone. I wouldn't be surprised if he has hired someone to follow me while I am here in Lexington. He's that crazy. I'm crazy. I walk in the door of our house and he's waiting for me. He's made plans for us to go to dinner with one of his friends tonight—I'm surprised he wants to be social. We get to the restaurant and dinner is great—we're all laughing and carrying on. His friend gets up to use the restroom, and I follow shortly after him. When I get back, Jack isn't smiling or laughing anymore. I don't know what's going on; I can't read him. We're lying in bed that night and we're not even touching. Suddenly he rolls over and taps my shoulder. I roll over toward him. He sits up—I guess he wants to talk about something.

"What was going on at dinner tonight?" he asks. I don't know what he means or what he's talking about. "You went back to the bathroom right after Paul. Did you try to fuck him, too?" he asks. You've got to be kidding me. This is ridiculous, really ridiculous. I don't even say anything. I roll back around, and tears start streaming down my face. I cannot believe this is my life.

The next day Jack leaves town for the week without telling me. I don't know where he is or who he's with. I start working on the save-the-dates for the wedding, and I just stop. I know this isn't going to happen—why am I even doing this? My wedding dress arrives in the mail the next day. I pull it out of the box and there's pink lipstick on the top of the dress; I know it's a sign. Warning—don't proceed any further. My friend Lauren visits me; she knows how much pain I'm in. I'm so lonely in Decatur, and the fact that she's willing to drive six hours to spend the weekend with me means so much. The weekend with her makes me realize I need to figure my way out of this. Lauren sees my pain and acknowledges it. She doesn't give me advice or tell me what to do, she listens to me. It was one of the most thoughtful and kind things anyone has ever done for me. I'm grateful.

The weekend is over—Lauren heads home and I assume Jack should be back at any moment. I get a text from him: "I will be home in a few hours. We need to talk." I don't know what to expect. Everything between us is unimaginable—honestly anything is possible. He comes home and we sit at the kitchen table. "We need to cancel the wedding. We need to slow down. We need to take some time apart," he says. I know it's the right thing to do, but I'm so scared. And I will do anything to avoid being abandoned. Anything. He ends up staying at his parents' house and I stay with mine. This is the beginning of the end. He says he can't trust me and I'm a liar and he doesn't even know who I am. He even has me convinced.

A week passes, and we need to decide if we're going to do this or not. I can't believe I quit my job and moved and changed my entire life for him. He is jealous and controlling and he's unbelievable. I haven't heard from him in seven days when I get a text from him. "Would you be willing to take a polygraph? That's the only way I will consider being with you," he writes.

My fear of abandonment overrides my judgment. "Sure, Jack," I say. "I will do anything to make this work." I don't even recognize myself. I tell my dad about it, and he thinks it's crazy.

"Vitale, you should never be asked to do that from someone you love," he tells me. And he's right.

I call Jack, "I'm not going to take a polygraph. You either trust me or you don't."

"Well, I don't trust you," he says. "Let's meet at Nana's house tonight at 6:00 p.m."

I get to Nana's house and I've left my keys at my parents', so I break into the house because I don't want to wait outside. I need to shower before Jack gets there because I smell like smoke. And he won't like that. I'm still at his beck and call.

I shower and get ready for our talk. I'm scared and I'm nervous—I'm all over the place. I don't know what's going to happen. I'm afraid it's going to be over. Jack arrives and we both sit down at the kitchen table. Jack looks serious, he starts talking, and it feels like he's rehearsed this speech a few times. "I think we need to end things between us before things get hostile," he tells me. Things are already hostile; what is he talking about? "I don't trust you and I don't know who you are."

I don't know what to say—I don't have it in me to fight anymore. I'm worn out. The conversation continues and we both get heated. "Well, you owe me money for the fertility appointments and our living expenses," I tell him. "You owe me half."

"I don't owe you anything," he responds. "Just keep the ring."

I'm angry and he's angry and I'm crying. We both get up from the table. It's over. This is it. I'm about the walk out the door, and I turn around. "I have one last thing I need to say to you," I tell him. "Don't you ever call another woman the names you called me. No one deserves to be called a slut or a cum dumpster."

"Well, you deserved it. You let enough guys shoot it in you."

I shouldn't be surprised by his words, but I am. I storm out the door. Those are our last words.

EIGHT
Rock Bottom

I'm now in Birmingham, a beautiful city but a lonely one. The days and months pass like Groundhog's Day: I wake up and take seven 30 mg XR first thing in the morning, sit outside and smoke two cigarettes, and get dressed for work. My outfits always consist of clothing that won't show my sweat stains. I can't wear colorful tops because they show stains more than lighter colors, so I stick to black or white to keep it safe. If I do wear a colorful top, I have to wear a blazer over it to camouflage the circles of sweat around my back and beneath my arm pits. After getting dressed, I might grab a few M&M cookies for breakfast. Then I head to work and smoke two cigarettes on the way.

Birmingham is ninety minutes south of where I grew up and seven hours south of what I always considered my real home, Lexington. Birmingham has rolling hills, a robust restaurant scene, and lots of wealth—very different from Decatur. I describe it as the southern Louisville—lots of micro-neighborhoods and restaurants and shopping. I like Birmingham because it's an escape for me—an escape from my failed engagement, my dramatic exit from Lexington, my family, and my past. It's like hitting the reset button except, then again, not really. I'm still abusing Adderall, I still work for lawyers, and I'm back together with Tom. I'm still up to my same bullshit; it's just a different setting. But I can pretend it's the reset button.

My apartment is the best thing to come from all this craziness. I live in the most charming historic home along Highland Avenue. The road winds between a landmark restaurant and beautiful homes and three parks. It's an amazing place to live alone, but it's still lonely. My apartment is the ground unit in a house broken into four units. It has its own back porch and twelve-foot vaulted ceilings, and a built-in bookshelf that takes up an entire wall of the living room. My apartment is what dreams are made of—honestly, I don't know how it fell into my lap. God must have felt sorry for me and gifted with me with something positive.

At work, I am laser focused and I forget to eat most days. In the afternoon, I take three to five more 30 mg XRs, depending on my energy level and workload. I try not to take Adderall past 3:00 p.m. because otherwise I am buzzing all night long. I leave work around 5:00 p.m. and, when I get home, I pour myself a bourbon and ginger ale. Sometimes I catch up with friends on the phone or do my obligatory check-in call with Tom.

Tom and I have been back together for six months now. After my engagement imploded, I was broken and needed comfort and Tom was the best immediate solution. In fact, I didn't skip a beat—it was as if my engagement and Jack never happened. Tom and I are desperate to make it work because we never had a proper ending to our relationship in the first place, no closure, no hard lessons learned that we could grow from and take into a new, healthier, more suitable relationship. We share much of the same rejection, judgment, and make the wrong choices together, and we are used to it. The Adderall use is the least of our concerns and Tom is good at not bringing it up, an avoidance I am comfortable and very familiar with. I am definitely using Adderall. In fact, I am using more than ever before. My addiction to Adderall, being thin, working, and perfection are in full swing.

After my first post-work cocktail, I will smoke a few more cigarettes and do a few more work things and then make another drink and order takeout for dinner. I will push food around my plate while watching reality TV. It is no way to live. Then after my third or fourth bourbon, I finally come down from the Adderall and am ready for sleep. Sweets are my favorite food group so I make my favorite ice cream dessert to eat in bed. This is my routine—always eat dessert in bed; being by myself in bed with a favorite sweet treat is indulgent and became my secret reprieve. I started doing it a few years ago at the height of my Adderall addiction when I discovered that I could eat whatever I wanted, whenever I wanted, and not gain weight. I would eat my treat in bed while watching reruns of *Sex and the City* or *Bridgette Jones's Diary*. This is my day on repeat. And I am fine because no one bothers me about my Adderall.

The only thing that is different is the number of prescriptions I can get my hands on, the number of doctors I can manipulate, and the number of pharmacies that will fill my prescriptions. I had been living and working in Birmingham for about five months when the worst snowstorm the city has seen in thirty years struck. People are stuck on the highway and some can't make it home, so they sleep at their offices and in their cars. Somehow, I am able to make it home safely, and luckily, I had gone to the grocery and liquor store the day before. I am fully stocked, except I only have two more Adderall XRs in my bottle. It looks like everything will be closed for the next two days. How am I going to fill my Adderall prescription? There's no way I can be stranded in my house, by myself, with no Adderall. First thing the next morning I start calling all the pharmacies and none of them are open. I finally find one Target store that is open for limited hours. The roads are terrible, and the city cautions people to stay off the roads. But I don't give a fuck. Filling my Adderall prescription is my top priority. I don't care if the roads are on fire or submerged in water—there could have been a tornado and I still would have ventured out. Adderall is my God and running out of it isn't an option—it isn't in my plan. And the snow is screwing up my plan. I start my car and drive cautiously on the roads. I am probably one of three cars I see on the road that day—both lanes are lined with stranded cars because the road conditions are so bad. It is a scene from the movie *Independence Day*. There is no life to be found.

My Adderall tolerance has reached its height. I am taking anywhere between ten to twelve 30 mg XRs a day. That is a total of 300–360 mg a day. Most people would have died from that amount—they would have had a stroke or heart attack. Not me—I just want more. I am seeing three different doctors at this point—Dr. 8 in Huntsville and Drs. 9 and 10 in Birmingham. Drs. 8 and 9 are post-dating prescriptions for me and Dr. 10 would only give me one prescription per appointment. It is open season. I am preoccupied with my drug habit. My time is spent waiting in doctor's offices, manipulating doctors for prescriptions, and waiting at pharmacies for my prescription refills. And the rest of the time I spend on work. Work and drugs. Work and drugs.

I can't get enough prescriptions to keep up with my tolerance. I wake up in the middle of the night with nightmares that police are knocking at my door to arrest me for doctor shopping and forging prescription dates. I live in constant fear. Fear that I will run out of Adderall. Fear of living a life without it. Fear of getting caught. Fear of gaining weight. Fear of a life of imperfection. I am scared—all the time. My ability to concentrate at work is failing—I am running out of Adderall and taking sick days to stay at home to detox. I am missing work, and when I am at work I am jacked up on Adderall and sidetracked making sure I have enough Adderall to make it through the week. I am running out of Adderall faster and faster and can't keep up.

I have no friends in Birmingham—I never thought I would stay there forever, so the idea of putting any effort into making friends seems useless. And I am never present anyway—during the week I am busy with work and Adderall and alcohol, and on the weekends I am either visiting Tom or he is visiting me. I am in a relationship that is loveless and convenient. We are together because we have been through so much—he is lonely, and I don't want to be alone. We are together because we only see each other every few weekends—and that suits me just fine. My relationship doesn't interrupt my Adderall habit or my routine. When we are actually together we drink all the time, which makes it easier for us to deal with each other or more accurately to deal with the fact that we know we are all wrong for each other.

After about ten months in Birmingham, I call Dr. 10 and leave him a voicemail asking for a replacement prescription because I have plowed through the prescription before it was due for refill. I tell him I have lost my prescription again—this is the second time I have used the same lie with this excuse with him so I don't know if it will work. I am terrified. The fear of running out of Adderall is all consuming. It has been a few hours and I still haven't heard back. I am scared. What if they find out? What if they turn me into the police? What if I can't get my prescription? I am crippled by fear. I open my phone and search in my contacts for one of my other doctors. I know I shouldn't press send to make the call, but the fear of running out outweighs the fear of getting caught. This is a dire situation. I only have two pills left and I already plan to take them in the afternoon. I need Adderall for tomorrow and the rest of the week. I press send on my phone and call Dr. 9 and leave a voicemail.

Finally, Dr. 10 returns my phone call, and, per my protocol, I screen his call to get ahead of the outcome and premeditate my response. He sounds angry in his voicemail. He tells me to call him immediately. My entire body grows tense and my chest is tight. I know what that voicemail means—it means he has found out. It means he knows I am seeing other doctors, and that means I could be in real trouble. He could call the other doctors and notify them or he could turn me into the police. I am scared out of my mind. I don't know what do, but I also don't want to run out of Adderall. I know something needs to change, but I am not ready.

Dr. 9's office returns my call and they tell me they have a prescription waiting for me at the front desk. Thank God. Thank God I will have at least a little more Adderall to get me through the next week or so. The only problem is that I don't know if I will be able to make it to the doctor's office in time before they close. They close at 5 p.m. and I have a meeting at 4 p.m. And then I am out of town the next day. I need to get my hands on the prescription. My 4 p.m. meeting ends, and I have fifteen minutes to make it across town in traffic. There's no way I can pull this off. I even call to see if they will stay open for me, but they say no and that I can get it in the morning.

I pull into the parking lot of Dr. 9's office at 5:15 p.m. I am late, but I am still going to try. Maybe someone will still be there working late. I look at myself in the rearview mirror of my car—I am exhausted from all of this, but I don't know how to stop. I jump out of the car and run toward the building. I walk in and the front door is open. I take the elevator to the second floor where the office is located. I run to the office door and pull on it and it is locked. There are windows around the door so I can see the front desk and the waiting area, and no one is there. I feel defeated. What am I going to do? There is some noise in the hallway—thank God, someone is here—maybe they can help me. The person turns the corner of the hallway pushing a cart of cleaning supplies. Maybe they will have a key to the office—maybe they can let me in. I ask the man if he can let me in and he shakes his head no. I am desperate. I need this Adderall today, right now. I look at God and plead—*just this last time, God. Please—just this last time.* If I can get one more prescription, I will stop—I promise. Even though I know it isn't true, I lie to God. I need the Adderall that bad.

I look through the windows one last time before I leave. I see someone locking up and walking through the reception area. Yes! Maybe this person can help me. It is another doctor that is leaving for the day. I step away from the door, so I don't scare him or catch him off guard. He opens the door and turns around to lock it and I approach him. "Hi there, I'm a patient of Dr. Nine," I say. "There's a prescription waiting for me at the front desk. Would you be willing to grab my prescription for me?" I continue to give him the abridged version of my sob story—I tell him I am going out of town and that I need it. It is ridiculous. He agrees and finds the prescription in an envelope marked "Vitale Buford." He hands it to me, and I feel instant relief. My prayer is answered.

* * *

It is coming up on Meghan's thirtieth birthday and all my friends are meeting in Nashville for her birthday weekend. I'm about to leave for Nashville and I realize I only have enough Adderall to last me one week, at best. I need to figure out my game plan—I still haven't returned Dr. 10's phone call—I am too afraid of the consequence. I try calling Drs. 8 and 9 to schedule appointments, but I haven't heard back. So, I am forced to ration my Adderall during the birthday weekend—I need to have enough Adderall to get me through the next week. I am more tired than usual and hungrier than usual because I don't have enough Adderall to keep up. We go shopping, and I try on a size four dress and it is tight on my hips. I look at my reflection in the mirror—I feel so fat and ugly and worthless. The Adderall isn't working like it used to—I used to be able to fit into a size two easily, and now a size four is tight. Fuck. I buy the dress anyway because I am determined to get more Adderall and lose more weight so I can fit into it. I am determined to feel worthy. I need that dress to fit me to feel good about myself. I want it to fit me perfectly. The rest of the weekend I am in my own world. I am there, but I am not present. I am consumed with fear about Adderall and the angry doctor and the uncertainty of my future. I don't know what I am going to do.

I am beyond desperate for Adderall, so I call Frankie. I dial her number and it feels like the phone is ringing forever. I'm hopeless. I don't know what I'm going to do. I hate asking my sister for drugs, but I need them, and she has them. "Hey sissy," she answers. Her affectionate response catches me off guard, but I'm just so grateful she answers. Thank you, God. Thank you, Frankie. I feel a glimmer of hope. "Hey, how are you?" I ask. We exchange pleasantries. I need to assess what kind of mood she's in. And I'm trying to buy myself some time before making my request. "Frankie, do you have any Adderall I can buy from you?" I blurt. "I'm in between prescriptions and I just need some to get me through the week." There's a pause on the other line. I don't know what she's about to say. My life is in her hands.

"I have some Adderall you can buy," she responds. I hate that she holds the power right now. I hate using my sister as a drug dealer. "I have ten 25 mg XRs you can have," she says. My anxiety is lifted. I can buy the Adderall from her on my way back to Birmingham. I leave Nashville early Sunday, telling my friends I need to get back for work. Frankie lives in a house that my parents bought for her a year ago. It is their attempt to help her get her life started over, especially with Bentley. But the house is just another enabling mechanism. I am not sure if I will see Bentley when I stop by. He is either with her or living with my parents or who knows where else. Her life is a mess—she is doing drugs, selling Adderall for money, barely taking care of her child, and not working. Thinking about her life is too much for me, which is why I avoid it, but not today. I need Adderall.

This isn't the first time I've called her for drugs. Sometimes I would reach Frankie on her phone (if she has paid the bill) and she would tell me to meet her somewhere to exchange Adderall for money, and then when the time came to meet her, she wouldn't answer her phone. I am hopeful, but it is always a fifty-fifty deal with her. I am almost to Huntsville and

I call her twice and get her voicemail. Damnit, Frankie. Please answer. I need my drugs. I keep calling and getting her voicemail—but I am desperate, so I stop by her house. She is there with Clayton; thank God. Bentley is there, too. I am buying drugs from my dealer, who happens to also be my younger sister. I give her $75 and leave.

I am holding on for dear life. I finally get back to Birmingham and I am overrun with depression. I check my mail and I have three letters—one from each of my doctors. Fuck. I've been in the game long enough to know that receiving certified mail from a doctor is not a good sign. I grab the three letters and go outside to smoke. I need to calm my anxiety before dealing with my reality. I need to calm down. I look at each letter—one from each of my doctors. A feeling of intense panic runs through my body. Anxiety is pulsing through my veins. My chest is tight. How did I let it get this bad? Is this the end of the road?

I open the first letter—it is from Dr. 10, the angry doctor. The letter states that he will no longer be able to be my doctor and not to contact him for future appointments. Whew—okay, that's not as bad as I thought it would be. But what if he calls the police? What if the cops know I am doctor shopping and changing dates on prescriptions? What if I go to jail? I will not be perfect anymore. I grab the letter from Dr. 9, my other doctor in Birmingham. The letter says that my doctor is no longer a part of their practice, and that I need to go elsewhere for care. And then the third letter—from my Dr. 8 in Huntsville. The timing of all three letters is not a coincidence—they have been communicating with each other. I open the third and final letter. It is a form letter, like the letter from the angry doctor stating he would no longer be my doctor. They have all gone through the motions and checked all the boxes to make sure they won't get in trouble legally. I am overcome with fear. My body is so tense I can't move. I can't feel. I don't know what to do.

I rock back and forth on the swinging chair on my porch. What am I going to do? How much trouble am I in? I sit back and slowly inhale the smoke from my cigarette and I hold it my lungs longer than usual. I take a deep breath and blow it out. Time is moving in slow motion. I grab my purse and take two 25 mg XRs. That means I have eight left, and I still have five 30 mg XRs from my last prescription. I lie to myself thinking I can take one pill a day, which will mean I have thirteen days left of pills. But in my heart, I know it isn't possible. I've taken thirteen pills in one day. If I control myself, those pills will last me three days at the most.

If I don't have doctors anymore, then I will find new ones. There must be someone that will prescribe me Adderall. I start googling and write down the names of fifteen doctors that I will call in the morning. I will call them first thing on Monday when they open. Okay. I am feeling hopeful now—and I have almost forgotten about the three letters. I go to bed that night drunk on bourbon and wake up to nightmares of the police knocking at my door. It isn't real, but I know that if my addiction continues—there will be real police at my door.

I wake up the next morning and take four 25 mg XRs, and I have four left. I start calling the doctors on my list, and I am able to get appointments with two of them—only two. The other thirteen aren't taking new patients or don't prescribe Adderall. I have to ask the question up front because I don't have time to waste. I go into work and I am exhausted and depressed. The life that I have been living for the past decade is falling apart. But I have a big event at my work, so I need to be on my game.

As the director of marketing and business development, I oversee professional development and training for attorneys. I have organized a firm-wide event and hired an executive coach, Justin, to speak to the attorneys about executive presence and body language. It is the first time we have paid an outside speaker to present on this topic, so it needs to be perfect. I can't mess this up. Fortunately, I have worked with Justin before at my firm in Kentucky, and I know how good he is. I pick Justin up from the airport—I am excited to see him; it is nice to see a familiar face. He presents to the attorneys in the Birmingham office, and then the Huntsville office—both presentations are a success.

Justin and I drive back to Birmingham from the Huntsville office—we have spent a lot of time in the car together today. We talk about life and our careers and love lives. There is a lull in our conversation. We have talked about everything possible at this point. "Would you mind if I ask you something?" he asks.

"Sure," I say reluctantly. His tone of voice is more serious, so whatever he's about to ask is beyond the context of what we've been discussing.

"Vitale, are you critical of your employees?" he asks. I am completely caught off guard by his question. Where did that come from? How could he criticize me like that? He doesn't know me. My face is getting warm—his question makes me angry and uncomfortable. I am silent. He must sense I feel attacked because he continues. "The reason I say this, is that I think you're critical of your employees because you're critical of yourself." I still feel attacked by his first statement; I don't know how to respond to this either. Who the hell gave him permission to tell me about me? He doesn't know me. He doesn't know if I am critical of my staff. It takes me a few minutes to calm down and hear what Justin is saying to me.

"Okay," I say. "Can you tell me more?" I don't want to know more but I also want to know why he's telling me this. "I observed your interactions with your staff today, and it just seems like you hold them to unrealistic expectations. Which tells me that you're holding yourself to unrealistic expectations," he explains. I'm not sure what else we discuss in the car ride. The idea of being anything less than perfect in my career has me feeling small and insignificant. We finally get to Birmingham, and before Justin gets out of the car, he turns to me and says, "I see in you what I refuse to see in me." I have no clue what that means but it haunts me.

I get home that night and I am beaten down. I am almost out of Adderall, Justin gave me advice I didn't want to hear, and I feel imperfect and uncertain. *I see in you what I refuse to see in me.* What the fuck does that even mean? And apparently, I'm critical of others because I'm critical of myself.

The only thing that is certain for me is uncertainty. My life is filled with uncertainty. A few days pass and I have gone through my Adderall supply. I divided the four 25 mg XRs and the five 30 mg XRs among three days. That's the best I can do. I wake up and have no Adderall. What am I going to do? And my mom is coming to stay with me for a few days—in fact, she will be at my apartment this afternoon. I go to work and try to hold it together. My mom is coming to visit me, and I am out of Adderall—great combination. I have a new doctor's appointment in a few days, so I tell myself I can handle two days without Adderall. Just two days. I've done it before, and I can do it again.

I leave work early to meet my mom at my house, and I am eager to see her. Everything going on in my life makes me crave my mom's love and attention. I feel so lost and alone—maybe spending time with her will take my mind off everything else? Maybe if I focus on her, then I don't have to focus on me. I pull up to my house and throw my cigarette out the car window. I take a few deep breaths. I want to see her, but I don't. It's always this way—I want to be with her, but then she ends up drinking and I regret spending time with her. Maybe today will be different—it's just the two of us for a few nights.

I walk inside my house, and as soon as I look her in the eyes I just know. She has been drinking. I am overcome with anger and hate and resentment. She is completely drunk. I know the look. She doesn't even have to speak; I can see it in her eyes. I am filled with rage. How could she come visit me and get drunk before I even see her? Doesn't she know I need her? I'm sick of being the parent. Doesn't she know I just want to spend some quality time with her? How could she do this to me? I just want my mom to be my mom. It has always been this way—always. I expect her to be sober, and I'm wrong. Her eyes never lie. Her tone of voice never lies. Her mannerisms never lie. I became a human sobriety detector at a young age. I learned to immediately discern my mother's state in front of friends when I was a teenager. I needed to know if she was going to be drunk mom or sober mom. I needed to know if I should prepare to be humiliated by her or if I could let my guard down. And her eyes became my guidepost.

"You're drunk!" I scream. I am filled with rage. "Why can't you just be sober? Why the fuck did you have to come to my house and drink? I just want to spend some time with you. All you do is think about yourself." My anger is all consuming. I don't know what to do with it. I grab the sides of her arms and look her in the eyes. "Why can't you just get sober?" There is a long pause. I let go of her arms and step back from her. My conversation with Justin pops into my head. *I see in you what I refuse to see in me.*

I am pointing the finger at my mom to get sober, but I, in fact, am the one who needs to get sober. I have been addicted to Adderall for a decade, and it just now dawns on me that I am the one who needs to change. Not her, but me.

The next day I ask my mom to leave—I don't really want her to leave because I don't want to be alone, but I don't want to be around her drinking. I need her here sober—my world is falling apart—and she can't promise me sobriety.

* * *

I lie in my bed and feel a level of exhaustion that I didn't think was possible, coupled with depression and hunger—it is all too much to bear. I call into work sick. The sunlight is shining in from my bedroom windows and it is bright. I was never someone who took naps or woke up late, so I never paid attention to how the sunlight comes into my room from the blinds. But it is bright—too bright. I am in a mood that calls for dreary weather like clouds and rain, not sunshine. I pull the covers over my head, attempting to block the sunlight. I still have the new doctor's appointment tomorrow, so that gives me some hope.

I arrive at the new doctor's office and I get a high crossing the threshold of the office. The possibility of getting Adderall has a placebo effect on me. I complete my paperwork and hand it over to the receptionist. I feel hopeful and cross my fingers. I need this prescription—just one more. I look up at God and plead for another prescription. *This is the last time, God—I promise.* The nurse calls my name and takes me back into the waiting room. I sit on the table lined with white paper. It makes crunching noises as I get myself situated. I am exhausted from the lack of Adderall in my system.

I tell the nurse that I am here to refill my Adderall prescription—I give her the same story I usually give at a doctor's office, but I am less hopeful this time. The doctor asks me the purpose of my visit as if he hasn't read my chart or gotten a summary from the nurse. So I repeat myself. He looks at me with the same poker face as the nurse—he is unresponsive to my request. I don't know what else to say—I don't want to come off as drug seeking, but I am also desperate for Adderall. "We don't prescribe Adderall in my office," he says. "It's too risky." Time seems to completely stop as those words roll out of his mouth. I won't be getting Adderall today. Holy fuck, what am I going to do? I have no other options. I have another new doctor's appointment scheduled, but they couldn't get me in for another month. My entire body tenses up, and I feel numb. I am in my body, but I am also out of my body—it is the strangest feeling. It is unreal. I want it to be un-real. My life has hit its bottom. I don't know where to turn. I beg the doctor to prescribe me Adderall and he declines again. I even show him my last Adderall bottle, and he still says no. There is no getting around this. I am done.

The events of the past few weeks are crashing in—my conversation with Justin, the visit from my mom, the letters from the doctors, running out of Adderall—it is all something I can't avoid any longer. I don't know where to turn. My body feels so heavy. I get down on my knees and start praying, *"God. Please help me deal with my addiction. Please. I will do anything. I don't want to feel this way anymore."* I am not praying, I am pleading for help.

I am now four days without Adderall. I am used to taking 360 mg of Adderall daily, and I am now on my fourth day without it. I am four days without Adderall. I can't handle it any longer. I need a fix. My sister says she has another prescription she can fill in a few days, and I can buy some from her. It isn't immediate relief, but it is relief. I feel guilty calling her only for Adderall, but I need it, so I stuff my emotions down.

It is day five without Adderall and I can't get out of bed. My depression and exhaustion are unbearable. I can't get up to go into the office, so I call in sick again. I wonder what my staff is thinking. They probably think I am faking it. I am so scared and so alone. Tom is on a college visit with his daughter and ex-wife, so he has no clue what is going on with me. No one has any clue what's going on with me. And I am not willing to tell him. Not yet. My parents keep calling me and I screen their calls. I can't fake that everything is okay—everything is not okay. And if I tell them the truth, what will happen?

I finally answer my dad's call. I'm at my breaking point. I need to feel not so alone. I need to tell someone I'm not okay. I need someone to know. "Are you okay, Vitale?" he asks. "You haven't been answering our texts and our calls; we've been worried about you." I stay silent for a few seconds and I start crying. I can't hold it in any longer. I am not ready tell him the truth, but I need someone to know I am in pain. I don't want to be alone in my pain any longer.

"I'm not okay, Dad," I say through my tears. "I'm depressed and something is really wrong." He asks what it is, but I'm not ready to admit it out loud. I'm not ready to tell him I am an addict. To say it out loud makes it real, and I'm not ready for real. I want to live in my fantasy world of denial for as long as possible. I don't want to let my dad down. It turns out he is driving back from Atlanta and will be passing through Birmingham. "Can I stop by and see you on my way home?" he asks. I agree.

I sit on my couch in silence. No lights are on in my apartment—the natural light is shining through my windows—except it is cloudy outside. There is a touch of gray reflecting throughout my apartment. Time is moving slowly. My dad said he would be here in forty-five minutes, and it feels more like three hours. I wait for my dad to arrive. What will I tell him? What should I say? I envision myself telling him about my addiction, but the shame and reality of it all is too much. I could make up some elaborate lie about why I am depressed, but it feels like too much work. I am sick of the lies and cover-ups and half truths. I am sick of living a double life.

My dad arrives and knocks on my back door, and I get up to greet him. It's the first time I have gotten off the couch in hours. I am still wearing my pajamas, and I have my blanket wrapped around me like a cape. He walks through the door and I hug him and start crying on his shoulder. I am crying uncontrollably. He doesn't know what to do with me or how to react. "It will be okay, Vitale," he tells me as he pats my back. But he doesn't even know what is going on with me—how can he know for sure that everything will be okay? How can he know that I will make it out of this alive? How does he know I will be safe?

He tries prying it out of me—not in an aggressive way, but in a concerned fatherly way. He wants to fix my sadness, and it can't be fixed. Not now at least. I don't feel like anything can fix the way I feel or what I am going through. The mountain seems too steep to climb. Thankfully it is Memorial Day weekend and I have an extra day off work, so I can wallow in my sadness a little longer. We are both sitting on my couch and I can tell he feels helpless. He's giving me this look of concern; he wants to help, but I'm not ready yet. "I'm not ready to tell you yet," I say. "I'm scared and I'm just really sad—really sad."

"Whatever it is, Vitale, we will get through it together," he says. He has no idea what's going on. He wouldn't be able to guess for a million dollars. I've kept my addiction a secret for ten years. And he can't promise me it will be okay. He doesn't know that for sure. I don't know that for sure. He offers to drive me back to Huntsville with him for the holiday weekend. I agree. I am in no shape to drive myself, and there is the hope of buying Adderall from my sister while I am there.

I know I will feel better if I can just get some Adderall in me. I promise myself that this will be the last time I ask her—if I can just get it from her this one last time. She tells me she doesn't have the money to pay for the prescription, but if I pay for it, I can have some of it. Deal. My depression starts to lift. I am at my parents' house waiting for my sister to pick me up. I tell my parents we are going to run errands and spend some "sister time" together. That should have been a dead giveaway that something sketchy is going on. Frankie and I as friends is never going to happen. But my parents are desperate for me to feel better, so they would've believed anything at this point.

Frankie and Clayton pick me up from our parents' house and we drive to the pharmacy to pick up the prescription. I feel so much relief in the car ride—I will have Adderall soon. Just a few more minutes and I will be me again. I need to feel like myself. This depression and exhaustion and anxiety are unbearable. I am barely able to function. I pay for the entire Adderall prescription and she gives me twenty 25 mg pills—they are the regular kind, not extended release like I was used to—but I don't care. Any Adderall is better than none at this point. Our drug deal goes down in the parking lot of the pharmacy. I pay for it and she gives me half of the pills. I want the whole bottle, but she won't give it to me. I settle for what I can get. I take three of the pills and feel better immediately. The placebo effect is a real thing.

I spend the rest of the holiday weekend at my parent's house. Since I have Adderall in my system, my depression isn't as severe. It is still there because I am on a much smaller dose. But it isn't as intense as the past few days. I ration the Adderall because I don't know when or how I will get my next fix. I don't want to think about that though; I just want to enjoy the feeling of Adderall in my system. I have energy and motivation and no hunger. I am not bloated, and I don't feel as fat. I am feeling like my old self again, back to perfection.

* * *

My mom drives me back to Birmingham since I don't have my car. Spending time with her when she is sober is what my heart craves, and she's sober right now. Even though I have Adderall in my system, I know I will run out soon, and that scares me. And I don't know where else I'm going to be able to get more. I've exhausted all options with doctors. I just need my mom. Being with her right now, sober, is exactly what I need. These moments are rare, but when they happen, they are special—it is like a carrot dangled for me in between her drunken episodes. Like my first night alone in my apartment in Birmingham—I felt so alone and lost, and I called my parents crying, and my mom drove an hour to Birmingham to be with me so I wouldn't be alone. Or the time my mom took me shopping for my college graduation dress or when they moved me to Lexington. Those were moments I treasured.

We walk into my apartment and I ask her if she can hang out with me for a little while. I feel so incredibly alone in my apartment by myself—if she can be there with me, it will be better. We both lay on my bed in silence like we used to as a family on weekend nights when I was a kid. We would pile onto my parents' bed and watch movies until it was time to go to sleep. It felt familiar; it felt safe.

The weight of my addiction floods my body. My chest grows tight and my entire body is tense. I know I can't live like this any longer. I know I need to do something about it. I know I have to change. I know there isn't an unlimited supply of Adderall. I am thirty-one years old, and I can't live like this forever. I can't do the doctor shopping, and pharmacy hopping, and pill popping anymore. I just can't do it. My hands tremble. I want to tell my mom my problem. She would understand. She struggles with alcohol, so maybe she won't judge me. Maybe she could still love me. Maybe I would still be lovable.

I look over at her and she is looking up at the ceiling in mid-thought. "Mom, I need to tell you something," I say. I get up from the bed and start pacing back and forth. "I need to tell you something," I repeat. She looks at me confused. She doesn't know what I'm about to say, but by the tone of my voice, it's serious.

"Okay," she says cautiously. She looks me in the eyes and her gaze makes me feel safe, "We can fix whatever is going on with you, Vitale. Everything will be okay." Her response feels warm and welcoming. I look her in the eyes. "I have an Adderall addiction. And I need to go to rehab for it," I say. I have prayed for this moment, and it is now here. I am finally dealing with my addiction. I am finally being honest.

She replies, "Okay, honey. Let's talk about this. We can get you help. Everything will be okay. Are you sure you need to go to rehab?"

"Yes," I reply. Suddenly sure and ready. "I need help."

NINE

Detox and Demons

I walk through my apartment one last time. I'm not sure what I'm looking for—it's not like there's a list of what to pack for rehab. But I want to make sure I don't forget the essentials—my phone charger, underwear, toiletries. I stuff two pairs of jeans and two pairs of shorts into my duffel bag, along with four or five tops and two sweaters, and only one pair of pajamas. I used to always pack my Adderall first, to be sure I would never leave it behind, but not this trip. This trip is different.

I turn all the lights off and lock the door. It could be anywhere from two weeks to twenty-eight days before I'd be back in my own bed. I'd leave it to the treatment experts to figure out how long it would take to fix me. And I assume they'll need more than a few weeks!

As I pull out of the drive-thru of my favorite fast food place to eat my last "normal" meal, I pull next to one of the outdoor trash cans. I remember hearing that they search your car when you arrive to make sure you don't have any drugs hidden in or around your car. I don't have any drugs, but I do have lots of empty Adderall bottles. They are stashed in the center console of my SUV—there are probably twenty or twenty-five empty bottles. I grab the bottles and put them all in an empty grocery bag—I'm disgusted by the number of bottles I have hidden in my car. I have a flashback to having people in my car—people I care about and who know me—like Meghan, Tom, Jack, my own parents—and being afraid they would open my center console and find out about my addiction. I tie the top of the grocery bag in a knot and I take one last look at it before I toss it in the trash can. It's freeing to not have anything to hide in my car.

The treatment center is in Warrior, Alabama, about a thirty-minute drive from my house. I won't be allowed to have visitors, and my phone access will be limited. I can write and receive letters, but the intention is to keep me focused on getting sober. The focus is on a new normal, a new sober normal.

While I am sitting nervously in the waiting room, a woman from the accounting department calls my name to finalize the financial paperwork for my treatment stay. I sign a bunch of documents and find out my insurance is covering all of my stay except for $1200. I feel relieved—I can afford that. I go back into the waiting area and wait another thirty minutes before a nurse calls me back and asks me to bring all my belongings with me. I'm about to have a psychologist evaluate my mental state, and then a nurse needs to comb through my belongings to make sure I don't have any drugs or alcohol or other prohibited items with me. Which I don't, but it still feels invasive.

They put me in a small room with a table and two chairs. I assume the other chair is for the psychologist. She comes into the room and she asks me thirty or so questions, evaluating my risk for suicide and my mental stability and clarity. I pass her exam and they slap a patient wristband on me—like I'm checking into a hospital. Which I guess makes sense. I have my own barcode and everything. They walk me down to the detox area of the treatment center and give me my room number. Everyone is required to stay at least one night in detox before they move to the cottages. I walk into my room and put my things on the empty bed. The other bed is occupied by my roommate who is sleeping. I've been detoxing for five days already so my symptoms aren't as bad. What I'm struggling with the most is depression, shame, and anxiety. After I put my stuff down, I am ushered to another room, so a cavity search can be conducted. They need to make sure I don't have any drugs hidden on or in my body. I am humiliated, but I deserve this. I deserve to be humiliated after all my lies and manipulation. And when you're an addict, people suspect you'll stoop to the lowest levels. They complete the cavity search and another nurse takes my vitals and bloodwork. This check-in process is thorough. Goodness. It's nighttime before they're finished with me.

I'm lying in my bed—the sheets are tough and feel like cardboard. They make a crunching sound every time I move, so I just lay still because

I don't want to wake up my roommate. At least the sheets are clean. It has been a long day, so I should be tired, but I'm not. I'm restless. I feel unproductive and useless. How long will I be here? What will my life look like after rehab? I have so many questions swirling around my brain, keeping me awake. The room is bare and plain. I get up and tiptoe to the bathroom; thank God, it's clean. I will be able to shower without flip flops. Everything is sterile and lifeless. I feel a conflicted sense of disconnect from everyone and everything I know, but I also feel a sense of freedom. I was a liar for a decade, at least. I lied about my drug habit. Friends would say, "How are you so thin? You eat and drink whatever you want, and you don't exercise." And I would reply, "Oh, it's genetic, I guess." This is total bullshit. I was cheating the system. Coworkers would say, "How do you get so much done and work all the time? How do you have all that energy?" I would reply, "I don't know. It comes naturally I guess." I lied and lied and lied.

And now I am confronting the lies that I used to hide the real problem: deep shame. I am confronting my demons and my struggle and my addiction to perfection, and I am hoping I'll have the strength to figure out where the shame stems from. I am confronting the void in my heart. I am confronting the lies and manipulation. I am confronting my past. It is freeing, but it is also daunting. I feel like a water faucet was just turned on—and I am flooded with emotion. I don't need to have it all figured out. But like any good perfectionist, I want it all figured out right now. Immediately. I want to deal with this "addiction thing" and move on. Let's check this off the list so I can move onto the next thing.

Day two arrives, and I wake up to the sound of one of the nurse's voices. "Wake up call," she says. "Time to get in line for your meds." It is 5:30 a.m.—a time of day I am unfamiliar with sober—I was only awake this early if I am out of my mind on Adderall and pulling an all-nighter for work or coming home from nights of binge drinking at bars with Jack. The medicines they have me taking are four or five vitamins. Most everyone else is prescribed much stronger drugs to help them detox from alcohol or cocaine or heroin.

I change out of my pajamas and into one of the five outfits I packed for rehab—I had no clue what I was doing when I was packing. I put on my clothes and brush my teeth and put my hair into a ponytail. I open the door in our room to walk into the main hallway and I need to squint because the lights are bright. I pause in the doorway and use my hand as a visor, waiting for my eyes to adjust to the bright florescent light that now jolts me awake.

Some of the folks are already in line to get their meds. That's part of treatment—there are four call times for medication—6:00 a.m., 11:45 a.m., 4:00 p.m. and 8:30 p.m. Each person has different needs—some people are taking drugs to help them safely detox from benzos or opiates or heroine; some folks are getting antidepressants; some folks are prescribed a combination of vitamins because their bodies are deficient from prolonged drug use. I am only prescribed vitamins, but I still have to wait in line with everyone else. It seems a little extreme to me, but I don't question it. They are the experts. They have us on a tight schedule for a reason—we need to develop a routine—something many of us lack in active addiction. "There's a reason why we do everything here," the nurses would say. "Trust the process." There's a reason for the early wakeup time, a reason we could only use the phone at mandated times, a reason for the meals they provided for us, a reason for the literature and classes they provided us. There is a reason for everything. I don't know the reasons, but I trust that they know better than me. Plus, I enjoy the routine and structure. It's what I lacked when I'd run out of Adderall and would call in sick to work. I didn't think it would be possible to have structure without Adderall, so experiencing it now is a good start.

After I take my vitamins, I go outside to smoke. There isn't much to do in detox except take your meds, smoke, eat, and read the Alcoholics Anonymous approved literature. I am addicted to stimulants—so "taking it easy" wasn't in my nature. I need constant distraction and busyness and activity. I need something to do to feel worthy. Down time was foreign to me. In fact—I was allergic to it. Being productive is part of my perfection criteria.

I venture upstairs to the cafeteria for breakfast. There are French toast sticks and bacon and eggs and cereal and yogurt and pancakes—all food I typically avoided. I don't usually eat breakfast when I am on Adderall—and in fact, the food scares me. I am afraid if I eat the French toast sticks that I won't be able to stop eating them and I will gain weight. That is my biggest fear of going off Adderall—gaining weight, being fat—being unlovable. Who would want to be with me if I gain weight? Today marks my seventh day sober and I am bloated and hungry and anxious and depressed. I want to eat it all. I am hardly ever hungry on Adderall and it takes my mind off food, which is one of the reasons I love the drug. I don't have to think about food or dieting or exercising. It turns all that noise off. And when I do eat, I eat whatever I want because it gives me the metabolism of a teenager.

I stare at the breakfast buffet for ten minutes. I don't know what to eat and I'm scared to eat. Food thoughts consume my mind, *Maybe I should just eat yogurt and cereal . . . oh, but the pancakes look so good . . . and what about bacon . . . but French toast and syrup is fattening, and I probably wouldn't be able to eat just one . . . I'm starving . . . I want to eat all of it . . . I should probably just skip breakfast . . . I could starve myself the next two weeks and lose weight—that would feel good . . . all it takes is one bite, and then my hunger is uncontrollable.* These are thoughts that go back and forth in my mind for ten minutes. I see other folks stepping up to the buffet line and getting whatever they want to eat. I wish it were that easy for me.

I finally step up to the buffet line and I pour myself a bowl of cereal—the healthiest of the three cereal options. I walk over to the cooler and I grab a low-fat yogurt and fat-free milk. I sit down at a table with two other women and introduce myself. We're all new to this rehab thing. I've picked up on the standard introduction that everyone uses—it's your name, how many days you've been in rehab, and your drug of choice. One woman is an alcoholic and the other one is a pain pill addict, and all three of us have been here under a week. Now it's my turn to tell them my addiction.

Upon hearing my addiction, everyone reacts to Adderall like it's Advil; like it's a joke, benign. Their eyebrows furrow as if they're confused. How can anyone be addicted to Adderall? Their mocking expressions make me want to defend my addiction, so I tack on alcoholism for good measure. If they only knew that I was taking upward of 360 mg of Adderall per day, they would take me seriously. I just want to belong.

I look at my food, and I'm scared shitless. I'm scared to gain weight. I'm scared of what that means. I begin eating and inhale everything on my tray—I even go back for seconds. *See, you proved yourself right, Vitale,* I think to myself. *You can't stop eating. Once you start, you can't stop.* I finish my breakfast and I want thirds, but I know better—plus I don't want people thinking I'm a glutton. I put my tray away and I head back down to the detox area. I lay on my bed for a few minutes and I'm antsy. I need something to do. I'm bored. I check in with the nurse about when I will be able to move to a cottage and they shrug their shoulders. There are four women in front of me waiting to move up to the cottages, so it might be a few days. I've already detoxed; I don't know why they can't just go ahead and move me up there. I'm probably more sober than any of the four people in front of me. It's so frustrating. I guess I just need to trust the process. There is a newcomer meeting in a few hours, so at least that will be something to do. I go outside and smoke cigarette after cigarette. I'm glad to be here but I feel so disconnected—from myself, from the people in this place, and from my friends and family. I wonder what's going on in the outside world. I wonder what my friends and Tom are up to—I wonder if anyone at work has even noticed I'm gone.

* * *

The next three days go like this: I wake up at 5:30 a.m. and get in the med line and then eat breakfast. Then I spend the rest of the day alternating between med line, eating, smoking, and laying on my bed. I'm anxious and I'm ready to move up to the cottages. There are two all-male cottages, one co-ed cottage, and one all-female cottage. The cottages are where the real work begins—you get assigned a counselor and you start learning tools and coping mechanisms for sobriety. I'm ready.

On day four of rehab, they finally have a spot ready for me in the all-girls cottage. Thank God. I load my belongings on the back of a golf cart, and one of the nurses drives me up to cottage four—the all-female cottage. Thank God I'm assigned that cottage, I think it would be weird to be in the co-ed cottage. I want to be around women—even if there are rumors that it's a sorority house and that all the women are catty. I surprise myself by being this relieved to be in the women's cottage. I've always been more comfortable around guys—not just vying for their attention—but as confidants, especially Matthew. *Oh, Matthew,* I pray. *Would I be here if I still had you in my life?*

I walk into cottage four. Some of the women are out back smoking; some are sitting on the couches in the living room journaling and napping. The air is humid and clear. I'm anxious about fitting in with this group of women, but I'm ready to do this. Plus, I hear you get a snack bag with all sorts of junk food and I'm all about food. I'm craving sugar. I introduce myself to the women in the living room, some of them smile and some of them look up but don't say anything. I just want to fit in. I go out back to smoke and my roommate from detox is outside—it feels good to see a familiar face. She motions for me to come sit next to her and she introduces me to all the other women—there are seven of them. I think there are sixteen or twenty of us total staying in the cottage. I light my cigarette and take the first puff and I feel more at ease. I think the other girls like me.

Everything they teach us here is centered on the Twelve Steps of Alcoholics Anonymous. In fact, I get my AA Big Book on my second day in detox—it's the main literature for the Alcoholics Anonymous program—it was written by one of the founders of AA, Bill W., and it helps guide you through the twelve steps. AA slogans are plastered all over the walls, and everyone refers to the Big Book. I always carry it on me because we read out of it throughout the day. In fact, some of the girls brag about which step they are on and discuss whether they plan on getting a sponsor after rehab. I don't know all there is to know about the twelve-step program, but I like what I know so far. I like the idea of growing closer to God (step three) and taking an inventory (step four) and eventually making amends (step nine). And the part of me that craves productivity, loves having the Twelve Steps as a framework and action plan for life. I like the idea of having a road map.

It's the afternoon and it's time for a Big Book Study—which is when we read out of the AA big book and then we go around the room and discuss it. We're in the middle of the group discussion when a young woman wearing an official photo ID motions for me to come over to her. She's my counselor—we're supposed to meet with our counselors throughout our time in treatment, and they are responsible for evaluating our mental health, our length of stay, and for recommending our recovery path after we leave treatment. I follow her up the stairs to her office. We both sit down, and we go through the standard intake questions—I'm so used to it at this point, I could recite the answers in my sleep. We start talking about my support network outside of rehab—who will I be able to lean on and who are my triggers. Well, my mom and my sister are my triggers. And the person who will be my main support is Tom, which is ironic since he was supposed to help me stay sober from Adderall the first time around with Dr. 3. She suggests facilitating calls with Tom and my dad to talk about my addiction and treatment and what kind of emotional support I will need beyond treatment. I don't know how it will go, or where things stand with Tom. And we identify two problems I need to work on during my time in treatment. My first problem is that I struggle with self-confidence and my second problem is that I need friends who support my recovery. We come up with short-term goals—most of them are journaling exercises to complete before I leave treatment. It's a lot of introspective work—work that I've been avoiding most of my life. But I'm a star student, so I can't wait to dive in so I can check it off my list. I love a good task list—I love things to do—I love being productive. Productivity equals worthiness and perfection.

One of the journaling exercises is all about setting boundaries with friends and family members after rehab to make sure I stay sober, which is about identifying who in my life may or may not be healthy for me. It's about looking at what and who I need to thrive in sobriety—and that includes the right people. I've heard the term boundary before, but I've never had one a day in my life. I could probably use some boundaries with my family, but that seems daunting right now. I'm asked to come up with example scenarios related to boundaries and how I would navigate dealing with people who are unhealthy for me. There are a few scenarios I can think of: when my sister calls me to borrow money, or when my grandmother calls me to complain about how my parents are treating my sister, or my mom's intoxicated complaints and comments about everything going on in her life. These are just a few of the scenarios in my life. It's interesting to identify them and put them on paper. And to identify them as abnormal and unhealthy—I thought it was just how families operated. And to step back and realize it's not normal—and that it's unhealthy—it was scary to identify. It was scary to think about creating boundaries—it was scary to think of all the drama and chaos I had surrounding me, and my role in all of it. I was responsible for a lot of it, including my self-imposed roles as the peacekeeper, the mediator, the hero, the rock. My counselor said that we teach people how to treat us—and that was an aha moment for me. Wow. I've been teaching people to walk all over me, to depend on me, to use me.

The other journaling exercises are more difficult than the boundaries exercise—which I didn't anticipate. It's the work I've avoided and the pain I've numbed for ten years. I'm supposed to write down memories that stole away my self-confidence and led to deep feelings of shame. I don't know where to start, so I pray to God to show me the answers, to give me clarity. So many memories start flooding my mind. Like the time I went to model tryouts when I was twelve and didn't get picked, or just my overall experience in middle school, which was a really difficult time for me. I was rail thin and wanted to be liked by all the popular girls who had boobs and hips. My body was a straight line, and I desperately wanted to fit in. Then there was my freshmen year of college when I didn't make sorority rush and I gained twenty pounds. Or the time I came home after a semester abroad my junior year of college, and I hung out with questionable people from my restaurant job and my mom called me fat. Or the time I was living with Jack in Decatur and all the emotional abuse. Or when I found out I had HPV my senior year of college and how much shame I carried around about that. These are all experiences I have minimized until now—I pushed them down with alcohol and eventually Adderall. I thought it was part of life—or just part of being human. To read these words and experiences on paper—to see them for what they are—to not minimize them—I start crying. I start crying for the hurt it caused me. I am overwhelmed, overwhelmed with all the awareness and trauma and change and sadness. I don't want to face this stuff. I just want to forget about it.

And then the floodgates really open. I can't stop thinking, writing, examining. The more it hurts, the more I write, and the more I write, the more I'd remember and write. The cycle makes me nauseous and exhilarated at the same time.

I remember memories in my mind, but I also feel them in my body, as I am reliving different pieces of my life. My body shame runs deep. It is deeper than my mom calling me fat, or my diet obsession, or my terminal weight loss and gains, or my insecurities in the bedroom. These are all symptoms of my deeply rooted body shame. But where did the roots start? How were they planted? What happened in my childhood that made me feel so inadequate and unworthy? These are questions my therapist and I set out for me to answer. My mom called me fat and then there were the mean kids in middle and high school—but we determine that my shame feeds my need for body perfection and body worthiness and thinness. I will do anything to be thin, to look like all the other women that have perfect bodies and perfect lives. Well, and I did. I was an Adderall addict for a decade. But this is all the aftermath of something much deeper, something much bigger. I don't know what happened, but my body knows something happened to me.

I can't pinpoint the memory—but I know something happened. Our body always has the answers. And I have been so disconnected from my body for my whole life. It's like I have my soul and then I have my body—and they are two different things. And since I see my body as something outside myself, it makes sense that I think it needs to be thinner and fitter to be loved. I need my body to shrink and disappear. I am obsessed. My therapist suggests there is a stored memory that I am unable to reach, but I can feel. I can't remember a lot of my childhood, but I know. I know that someone must have molested me or something, but I don't know where to turn to uncover this information. I could ask my mom, but she'd either deny it or drink over it or both. And then there's this idea that if it has happened, I should be able to remember every single detail, right? I should know. I should be able to remember. Maybe I'm just making this up or being dramatic? I don't want to be a victim.

I push it back. I don't tell anyone, especially not my therapist. I just think about it. I think about all my sexual encounters—how uncomfortable I was. How I only want certain parts of my body touched or seen. The oddness I feel around girls kissing and touching. How I am constantly judging myself with my clothes off—and my clothes on. It's why most, if not all, of my sexual encounters happen when I am intoxicated. I need to be numb when it comes to sex. I flashback to some of these moments and I grimace. It was terrible. I was terrible. I am gross and unworthy and unlovable. I just allow my body to be used. And I drink because I don't want to feel. I don't want to feel a damn thing.

But how did I arrive here? I can't pinpoint it. Not yet at least. The trauma is stored in my body—but my body is separate from me. It might as well be its own person—a stranger—because I sure as hell don't know her. I don't know this stranger. I don't know what she wants or what she needs—I only know that she knows something happened. It is a secret she is keeping from me—maybe for my safety and survival, maybe to play some sick joke on me. Either way, she isn't telling me. But I am writing my memories on paper and I can't escape it any longer. I close my journal and go out back to smoke.

The rest of treatment is routine. We wake up at 5:30 a.m., take our meds, attend group therapy sessions, see our counselor, meditate, journal, and smoke. Each night at 8:00 p.m. we all go to the cafeteria for a speaker meeting—where someone in recovery or a group of people speak about recovery. There is a different speaker each night and we all sit and listen and take notes, as the guest speaker shares his or her story of sobriety and what life is like for them now. And then 9:00 to 11:00 p.m. is our free time; it is also our opportunity to use the phone.

On day nine during the evening speaker meeting, I am reading the latest letter from Tom. He is saying how he is confused about our future and how he can't get over what I did to him with Jack. That letter is my breaking point. Here I am, fighting for my life, uncovering all these memories from my past, hating myself for the things I've done, and trying to get better and recover what I have done to my poor body and soul. And all Tom is concerned about is San Francisco, and the things that happened a year ago. Really? This, from a man who is old enough to be my father! I feel so lost and alone, yet I'm doing the work to change, to do something different. All Tom can think about is himself.

In the middle of the meeting, I start crying uncontrollably. It feels so futile. I can't stop my tears, so I run out of the cafeteria onto the front sidewalk. I need fresh air. I want out of this fucking place. I can't handle it anymore. I have zero contact with the outside world, I am facing my demons, I am surrounded by drug addicts and alcoholics, and I want out. I want to flee. I want to take back my admission of addiction. I want my Adderall back and my life back and my body back. I want my normal life back. I don't want to face my past—I want to hide from it. Tears are pouring out of my eyes. I crouch down to the ground and hug my knees and bury my head between my knees. I don't want anyone to see or hear me. I want to disappear. After ten minutes of this, the two head counselors from my cottage approach me. They ask me what is wrong and help me up from the ground. I am still crying and can hardly talk through my tears. "I just want out of this place," I say, sobbing. "I feel suffocated. I don't know how I can be here for another week or however long I'm supposed to be here."

"This feeling is completely normal," says one of the counselors. "Everyone has a meltdown on either day seven or nine of treatment. It's completely normal."

Just hearing that gives me relief. *Oh, okay*, I think to myself, *this is normal*. I'm not out of place. Everyone freaks out, everyone has an identity crisis, everyone is uncovering memories, everyone realizes who their real life supports are, and everyone realizes their own weaknesses and strengths. The strengths are what scare me. My tears start dissipating and my breathing calms down. I calm down. I hug both counselors and head back into the cafeteria for the rest of the speaker meeting. I can handle this. I can do this. I can do hard things. *Don't be afraid of your strength*, I think.

* * *

My dad writes me the sweetest letter about how proud he is of me for taking this step to get sober. "There are followers and there are leaders, Vitale, and you are definitely the latter," he writes. I guess I am a leader. I've never been afraid of risk. Hell—I lived a risky life for ten years—doctor shopping, forging prescriptions, and manipulating doctors. But it feels good to hear it from my dad. It feels good to get praise for taking a major step. I junk the letter from Tom.

On day ten of treatment, I am voted chairperson of the cottage—which means I lead all the meetings, assign all the chores, and generally keep the peace in the house. I love being the chairperson—I love the power, and leadership comes naturally to me. I love being the favorite. It gives me value and significance. It also keeps me busy. We have chore time each morning during which we can watch TV. We turn the channel to the music videos and dance during our chores. It feels good to act silly and laugh and not be so serious. I spend so much of my life being serious—and I am done with that. Adderall is all about being serious and getting shit done. I want to learn how to *be*. One of the songs plays over and over each day and it becomes my mantra for sobriety—it is "Ain't it Fun," by Paramore. Some of the lyrics really speak to my new reality "So what are you gonna do when the world don't orbit around you? So what are you gonna do when nobody wants to fool with you? Ain't it fun/Living in the real world . . ." Ha. I used to think the world revolved around me. Those lyrics really stick with me. The real world—a sober world—is my new reality. It's my new normal. But so are the memories stored in my body, and I know that my treatment on the "outside" means continuing the hard work on the inside. My recovery is just beginning.

TEN

Early Sobriety

After fifteen days in rehab, the day comes when I am ready to check out: Friday, June 27, 2014. I am ready to go but I am also scared to leave my protective bubble. How will it be in the real world? Will I be able to perform at work? Will I gain a ton of weight? Will my friends still like me? Will I still be employed? What is going to happen with Tom and me? I have so many questions. Leaving treatment is bittersweet.

It is 10:00 a.m. and I am ready to go. I grab all my stuff and walk down the hill to the main check-in area. As I walk out, Tom is waiting for me. I can't wait to see him, to feel close to someone, not to feel so lonely. I need his presence. I run toward him and we embrace and hold each other tight. He tells me I look good, which is nice for me to hear since I am so afraid of how much weight I gained during rehab. I go through the checkout process, and they give me the clear bag that holds my keys and my phone and my purse. I am grateful to have some control back in my life. I am grateful for my car keys and my phone, and access to the outside world.

Tom gets in his car and I get in mine to follow him back to my apartment in Birmingham. I start my car and roll down my window and light a cigarette. I feel so grateful to be going home and to return to real life. We get back to my house and Tom wants to hear all about treatment—he wants all the details. This is typical of him, always wanting me to share my life, but never sharing his. But I am not ready to share my experience with him. I still haven't processed it myself. I want to tell him, but it's hard to even put in words or explain. It's hard to explain sobriety to someone who isn't sober. At least for me it is. I want to share with him, but I don't want him to ruin it for me. I don't want him to take away from my experience.

I immediately feel the distance and strain and resentment between us. It was there before I went to rehab and it is still there. I was hoping it had gone away but it didn't. And because I am sober, I am more aware of it than ever before.

It is Friday night and Tom made reservations at some fancy Birmingham restaurant. I can tell he wants to return to life as usual. But I am not the same person. I need time to adjust. I need time to figure things out. I need time to process. He wants to skip right over rehab, pretend it never happened and for everything to be business as usual. He makes himself a martini and then he makes me a bourbon. I am not ready to drink alcohol—I haven't made my mind up yet about drinking. I reflected on my alcohol use during treatment, and I uncovered that it is more of a problem than I had realized. Couldn't he just wait—couldn't he just go one day without drinking?

When I was on Adderall, I could drink most people under the table since my body was metabolizing the alcohol faster. And then for the last four years, I was drinking every day. And I'm not kidding—every single day for the last four years. That's 1,460 days of consistent drinking—and I'm talking bourbon. Like two to four bourbons a night. It's hard to say that out loud and pretend like alcohol isn't a problem. In treatment they encourage you to abstain from all substances. They say that if you start drinking, you're likely to go back to drugs. And I don't want to go back. I feel the pressure from Tom to continue drinking, but I don't give in. I can feel his disappointment. It makes me angry that he wants me to drink. We had discussed my abstinence from substances with my counselor at the treatment center, and yet here he is being the opposite of supportive. I feel so small and insignificant. I feel so alone and lost.

* * *

My first day after rehab is a mix of emotions. I feel like I have to put on a show for Tom instead of just processing and being present. I need to go to AA meetings and focus on my sobriety, and he wants to drink and pretend like everything is the same. I have strict instructions to follow: I am going to start my outpatient treatment on Monday, I am going to attend Twelve-Step program meetings like AA on the days I don't have outpatient, and I need to get a sponsor. I don't want things to be the same. I am a new person, and that means a new normal and new way of living. I have a sobriety task list, and I want to get things done.

Tom returns to Lexington and I return to my life in Birmingham. My friends in Kentucky are ready for me to move back. But I don't even know who I am. I feel so lost and confused but also free. Free to be honest and no longer hide behind my drug addiction.

The next weekend is the Fourth of July, and Tom and I are meeting my friend Lauren and her boyfriend at Bald Head Island for the holiday weekend. This trip was planned way before I decided to get sober so there is no backing out. I am nervous and anxious because I know there will be a lot of drinking—I am not bothered to be around it—but I am afraid I will cave in and drink with them. I am still on the fence with my decision to drink and I am only six days out of rehab. I have no idea how it is going to turn out. Tom wants me to drink, and I'm sure my friends think it will be fine for me to drink, too. "You aren't an alcoholic; you're an Adderall addict—why wouldn't you drink," I can hear them saying to me. I don't want to go, but I had made the commitment, and everyone is expecting me to show up. Everyone is expecting me to be the same person—but I'm not. I'm not the same at all. I'm naked and vulnerable and green and hopeful and scared shitless. What will it mean if I drink—will that erase my sobriety? Will I have to start over? I am thirty-seven days sober and I don't want to ruin it. I don't want to feel the guilt and shame all over again—I have enough of it already—I don't need more.

I don't know what I am going to do. I am nervous and I am anxious. Tom and I are on the way to Bald Head Island, and like any good early sobriety person, I have all my recovery literature with me. I have three meditation books, my journal, and the Big Book. I am still on my pink cloud of sobriety, feeling hopeful and optimistic about my future. I don't have a sponsor yet, but I do have a network of people I have met in rehab and at meetings. I can reach out to them if necessary. We finally get to our friend's house and there is a hurricane looming. All restaurants and grocery stores are shut down because of the bad weather. We are literally stuck in the house—with little food and a lot of alcohol. It is my old version of heaven and my new version of hell.

When we get to the house—they want to hear all about sobriety—what it was like in rehab, what the days were like leading up to my sobriety . . . why I think I have a problem. I feel like I am being interrogated by the police. Like there is a spotlight on me. And I don't want to be in the spotlight.

I start telling them everything—and it turns out it feels good to be so open and free. It feels good to be honest for a change. Tom is bored with the conversation—he has already heard everything and lived it—he is ready to move past it all. He is ready for it to go away. But it isn't going away. It is here to stay. I am committed to my sobriety. My friends press me about my drinking—trying to convince me that I don't have a drinking problem. I remember my therapist in rehab talking about people who aren't healthy and boundaries, and this wreaks of one of those scenarios . . . I am torn. I don't know what to do. I feel cornered.

That afternoon I make the decision to drink. I'm not proud of it. I just want to belong; I want to feel normal. I want to fit in. Tom, Lauren, and her boyfriend are all drinking and having fun—and I want to be a part of it. So I cave. I feel like a foreigner. I have just gotten out of rehab and I am stuck in a house—literally stuck—and I can't leave. I can't breathe. I can't get centered in all the noise. I have just spent fifteen days in a treatment center and I have worked hard for thirty-seven days of sobriety and now I am drinking. "Of course you're drinking . . . now you have to start over . . . you've ruined your sobriety . . . you can't tell people you're sober anymore because you drank . . . you're a bad person . . . you have no willpower . . . you're not perfect . . . ," all of these thoughts are racing through my mind. My fear of gaining weight is too loud. I already feel fat and ugly—bourbon will just make me gain more weight. And I am hungry now. Fuck. Of course, I am.

The evening goes on and I end up drinking three or four bourbons. I haven't had any alcohol in thirty-seven days, so I am buzzed. And I am angry. I am irrationally angry—at Tom for not supporting my sobriety, at my friends for not understanding—but mostly I am angry at myself. How could I do this? How could I throw away thirty-seven days of hard work? How could I fuck this up so soon? I know alcohol isn't my drug of choice, but I want to be the perfect person in recovery—I want to follow the rules perfectly. I want to do the step work perfectly. I don't want to mess it up or misstep. I want to get it right from the beginning. And now I can only say I'm sober from Adderall—not alcohol.

That evening Tom and I get in a huge argument—I know it is the beginning of the end. I am still in denial but deep down I know. He wants to have sex and I want nothing to do with it. I just want to be left alone. I am in too deep with guilt and shame. He gets so angry at me for not having sex with him—he yells and screams and blames me for every-thing—for Jack and for his job and his divorce. And I shut down. I can't take it. I am drunk and in a miserable relationship, and, behind the scenes, I am completely covered in shame. I am a bad person for drinking. I am a bad girlfriend. I am bad. I have just left treatment—can't he give me some grace? Or a fucking break?

* * *

When I get back to Birmingham, I recommit fully to my sobriety—no drinking, no Adderall, no nothing. I am more committed to living alco-hol-free because of my fear of gaining weight. Whatever the reason doesn't matter—what matters is being a perfect sober person. There are 404 miles between Tom and me. And I am grateful for the distance—it allows me to be detached and free of him. I can live in my own bubble and focus on my recovery.

I visit Lexington and Tom a few weeks later because it is "my turn" to visit. He has been doing all the driving and leg work, so I need to try—well, at least appear to be trying. I don't want to—but I also don't want to rock the boat. There are too many other moving pieces in my life—I am trying to figure out life as a sober person—I don't want to deal with a breakup right now. I am redefining myself and my life. I am figuring out my professional life as a sober person, I am figuring out my friendships as a sober person, I am figuring out my daily routine, I am figuring out my body and my food and everything. Adderall allowed me to work until two or three in the morning, and that isn't possible for me anymore. Who I am professionally—that scares me the most—I don't know if I can be as successful in sobriety. I am used to eating whatever I wanted on Adderall and that is no longer the case. I am an entirely different person on Adderall, and I have been that person for a decade. And it is now time to reinvent myself. I am relearning how to live. I am calmer and more present and settled in sobriety. I like it, but I am not used to it.

I arrive at Tom's house and—big surprise—he is already drinking. Of course. When I was in treatment, they had a class for friends and family of people in recovery. It was a class that taught them how to be supportive of our sobriety. I asked him to go—but he didn't make the time—he was too busy. I even asked him to attend some Al-Anon meetings—but he dismissed the idea. I need him to support my sobriety. And that means not drinking all the fucking time. I want to have sober conversations with him about my sobriety—imagine that.

We go to dinner at a new restaurant in downtown Lexington that evening—Tom is already three martinis deep—and I am sober. The restaurant is packed so we sit at the bar—of course we end up sitting at the bar—how poetic. He orders himself a drink and then he looks at me. I order water and tell the bartender that I need time to think about my drink order. Tom goes on his diatribe about me not being an alcoholic. "Your mother is the alcoholic . . . stop thinking you're anything like her—you're not . . . quit making your addiction into something it isn't . . . quit pretending to be an alcoholic . . . your problem is Adderall, not alcohol . . . ," he goes on and on. I am so sick of it, sick of his bullshit and complete lack of understanding and awareness. I order a glass of white wine to shut him up. I can't listen to him anymore. And maybe he has a point. Maybe I'm making this alcohol thing a way bigger deal than it needs to be. Maybe he knows what's best for me. I think ordering wine will be better than bourbon—less characteristic of an alcoholic, which of course is totally alcoholic behavior: to order a "less bad" type of alcohol. Ugh.

I take two sips of the wine and push the glass away from me. I am filled with shame—shame for not having self-control, shame for giving in, shame for putting up with his bullshit, and shame for once again not being perfect. I am done with drinking. I can't handle the guilt and shame that come with it. It is my last drink—a bullshit glass of white wine.

The distance between Tom and me grows. I do my own thing in Birmingham and he does his own thing in Lexington. We are together out of obligation. I resent him for drinking, and he resents me for not drinking.

After my last drink, I am laser focused on my recovery. I am not letting anyone, or anything, take it away from me. I go to work at 8:00 a.m. and then I go to intensive outpatient treatment from 6:00 to 9:00 p.m., four days a week. And on the other days, I split my time between Alcoholics Anonymous meetings, Cocaine Anonymous meetings, and meetings with my sponsor. Work and recovery are all I have time for, and I am committed to my sobriety. My life in active addiction was miserable—there is no way I am going back to that. So whatever they tell me to do, I am doing. If I need to go to meetings and outpatient and work with a sponsor and journal and read recovery literature—well—I am doing it. I like my freedom in sobriety, and I don't want it taken away.

* * *

There are a lot of interesting things I discover in early sobriety. First, I have a ton of free time. I have spent so much time going to doctors' appointments and filling prescriptions and I now have all this time. It is scary. It is almost too much time. I now have time to think about my past, time to focus on my recovery, time for introspection. I keep journaling, which I find to be a great gift I left the treatment center with. Those earmarked issues about my shame and the emotions I physically felt in parts of my body need to be explored. Journaling coupled with my outside therapist, who was also my last psychiatrist in Kentucky, Dr. 7, are my two plans to keep nudging those demons free.

Another thing I discover is that I am more productive sober. Adderall made me an intense maniac. I was chain-smoking and writing task lists, but I wasn't getting a lot done. I am more efficient in sobriety, which is a surprise to me. I was so afraid that being off Adderall would negatively affect my performance at work, but it improves my performance at work. I get the work done, without the mania.

I also discover that I am on time for everything in sobriety. On Adderall I was always late—and I mean always. I didn't care about anyone else but me; I was on Vitale time. My clocks were set fifteen minutes ahead during active addiction because I was chronically late. But in sobriety I am right on time, all the time. It's like I have respect for other people's time and schedules. I am thinking about people other than myself for a change.

My sponsor, Carrie, is a twenty-two-year old recovering heroin addict. She is ten years younger than me, but I am drawn to her. She is very involved in AA and she is friendly and knows everyone. And she is approachable. I need approachable, as it is scary to ask someone to sponsor me. What if she says no? I need to find a sponsor to guide me through the Twelve Steps. I need that accountability and guidance. I ask her to be my temporary sponsor—that way neither of us have to commit right away. I want to make sure we mesh well together. She accepts the role of temporary sponsor and we meet for the first time at a coffee shop. I walk into the coffee shop nervous, not knowing what to expect. I am going to meetings regularly and I am still involved in my outpatient program, which requires me to attend evening meetings four days a week—but I am still nervous. What if she doesn't like me? What if she decides not to sponsor me? What if my addiction isn't bad enough? I am a successful marketing director at a law firm with a former Adderall habit—what if I'm too bougie for her? So many questions are swirling around in my mind. I take a deep breath and find a seat. We both put our books and journals on the table. I can't believe we are being so out in the open with our recovery materials—what will people think? Carrie couldn't care less if people see her with her Big Book. It is refreshing to be out in the open with my sobriety. She walks me through the process of doing step work. I just want to push through and get it done. Let's do the first, second, and third step right now. But she doesn't let me. We read a few passages from the book together and we pray—right out in the open in front of everyone. We do my first step together. She gives me some homework and reading to do before we meet the following week, but it feels good to be making progress, to be a straight A student in recovery. I'm going to do this perfectly.

One of my homework assignments is to write a list of fifty ways my life is/was unmanageable, which is no easy task. I struggle with understanding unmanageability because my life on Adderall was under control—at least on the surface. I had the perfect body and the perfect job. My outsides were perfect, but my insides were far from that. My insides are imperfect. I am in a relationship with a man twenty-seven years older than me and I am no longer attracted to him, yet I am staying in the relationship out of fear. The range of emotion I can experience in the span of five minutes is astonishing. I have shut off my emotions for so long, and now I am drowning in them.

And then there is my family's drama and chaos—I am still as codependent as ever and in the eye of the storm. My fear of gaining weight runs my life—and I am obsessed with eating the right foods and getting back into exercise—something I never had to worry about in active addiction, but I am all too familiar with. There are so many ways my life was unmanageable in the past and still is in the present, but I struggle with connecting the dots. It is an oxymoron—being a control freak leads to unmanageability. It's like I need to be out of control to be in control. I pretend to understand the concept because I want to move through the steps as fast as possible. I want to check it off my list.

* * *

There are upsides to early sobriety and there are downsides. I have gained about thirty pounds in the first four months of sobriety, which is a complete mind fuck. My body image issues rise to the surface and consume me. After I complete my outpatient program, I have time for exercise. And that's what I do. I move from Adderall to exercise. I try every type of exercise and every kind of diet. I want results, and I want them fast. But I don't consider the fact that ten years of Adderall really messes with your metabolism. My metabolism is used to having a drug run the show, and now the drug is gone, and my metabolism is slow. It doesn't matter how little I eat or how much I exercise—I can't get the weight off. It's all I think about. I am obsessed with my weight. I hate my body and I feel hopeless and defeated.

I move onto steps four and five—the steps where you take an inventory of yourself and all the things you fucked up, and then you admit all that to another human being. In this case I admit them to Carrie, my sponsor. She even has me come up with a list of all the people I've slept with—not a fun list to put together. I can't remember some of the names of the guys I've slept with, so I just put "chef" or "musician." Looking at that list is difficult for me. My period of promiscuity is one of the most shameful times of my life. I was really hurting and looking for love, and so I slept with a lot of guys. I guess it's all relative—my sponsor says my list is short. There are sixteen people I can remember—emphasis on "remember." All of this is part of the process: looking at our behavior and the motivations behind our behavior—the hurt and trauma behind our behavior.

I am sleepwalking through the steps. I am only willing to do the steps at a surface level. And I am only doing the steps because that's what everyone is told to do. I am not ready to look at the damage and destruction I have left in my wake. I attend AA meetings, but it doesn't quite fit. AA welcomes all addictions, but you have to identify yourself as an alcoholic. And I don't identify as an alcoholic, I identify as a drug addict. I remember one of my first AA meetings, when we went around and introduced ourselves, I said "Hi, I'm Vitale and I'm an addict," and the looks I got from other people in the room made me feel like an alien. From that point on, any time I go to AA meetings, I go with "Hi, I'm Vitale and I'm an alcoholic." It feels inauthentic. I abused alcohol, but Adderall was always my true love. I feel so misunderstood—I feel like Adderall addiction should have its own Twelve-step program. Adderall is different than alcohol and other drugs. I used it for perfection. And it is an invisible drug—you look perfect on the outside, but you're struggling in silence on the inside. The person I hurt the most through all this is me. And when it comes to making amends I am uncertain. I decide to make amends to my parents, my sister, Tom, and a few friends.

I haven't stayed in touch with Frankie, but I hear about her through my parents. Her drug use has escalated—there is a warrant out for her arrest in another county and she's been stealing jewelry from my mom and pawning it for cash. The events of her life are dramatic, and I honestly don't want to know what's going on with her because it hurts too much. She's still married to her second husband, Clayton, but Bentley is with my parents most of the time. My parents want to make sure he is safe—I want to make sure he is safe. Hearing about my sister is much different now that I'm sober. I feel so much sorrow for what's she's going through and the drugs she's using to try to escape her own pain. I feel sorry for her, and I also resent her for the chaos she causes—and she's always the topic of conversation with my parents. She sucks all the energy out of the room. I need to make amends to Frankie, but I also need her to be sober when I do it—and that will be tricky.

My opportunity comes after Frankie spends thirty days in jail for a drug bust. I pick her up from jail and make amends to her the next morning because I know she's sober and I want this to be a clear conversation. I want both of us to remember it. "Frankie, I want to make my amends to you if that's okay," I ask. I am nervous—all the pain and hurt I've caused her can't be ignored any longer. "Sure thing, sissy," she responds. "I'm sorry for using you to buy Adderall, and I'm sorry for my behavior on your wedding day." I go on and on about how sorry I am. It makes me sad to think about our relationship—or lack of relationship. She is five years younger than me—she is getting out of jail for the second time, she has a son she can't take care of, she doesn't know how to function without a man in her life, and she can't hold down a job. Being too connected with her gives me deep sorrow—a sorrow I am not ready to feel. I make my amends and move on, but I can't shake what I've done to her. I can't shake the fact that the only relationship we have is based on Adderall—I only called her when I needed it. I thought I was better than her, but we are more similar than I want to admit. She just wants to be loved and I continue to reject her. She is very manipulative and every time I try to get close to her, she burns me, badly. I cut off my emotional attachment to her—I have to for survival. To think about her life is too painful for me.

* * *

I finish all Twelve Steps in a matter of months, and I am happy to check them off my list. Done. Now I can move on. The amends I make aren't real. I am not taking this process seriously—I take my sobriety seriously—but it doesn't quite fit with my Adderall addiction. I need someone to understand my need for perfectionism—and how deeply it runs through me—it courses through my veins. They say that all addictions are the same—we're all using drugs and alcohol to cope with our wounds and that our addiction is merely a symptom of deeper issues. I believe all of it but the idea that all addictions are the same. They aren't. Society tells you to be perfect and productive and that's what Adderall gave me.

My first ten months of sobriety are monotonous. I go to work, I exercise, I work on my recovery, and go to meetings. That is it. That is my life. But it's what I need to make it through my early recovery. My emotions are all over the place. Somedays I feel happy to be sober, and other days my emotions are too much to bear. I used Adderall and alcohol to cope with my feelings, and now those things are gone. I feel naked with my emotions and my past. I can't un-see the things I've said and done—and some days it is more than I can bear. Somedays just getting out of bed and going to work are an act of courage. Somedays the best I can do is to call my two girlfriends in sobriety and tell them I need to complain. Somedays I binge on TV and food to distract me from reality. I am a roller coaster of emotions and feelings—but that's part of it. Emotional sobriety is way harder than substance sobriety.

Everyone in Kentucky wants me to move back, me included. But I am scared. I had destroyed so much when I left abruptly two years ago. It is embarrassing to visit Lexington and go out in public. Some people congratulate me on getting married and I have to tell them that my engagement ended. Some people see Tom and me out and wonder why or how we are back together. Other people are just excited to see me, but I am so embarrassed. I am uncomfortable with my past—how I left things, how I treated people, how I acted. The person most uncomfortable is me. I desperately want to move back, but I am paralyzed by fear and judgment. And I don't know what I want to do professionally. I never had to look for a job—I was always recruited by companies, so job searching is new for me. I need to update my resume, and even that I struggle with. I know I need a change—a major change but I am paralyzed with fear.

I keep in touch with Dr. 7, my psychiatrist in Kentucky, because he really knows me. He knows me as an Adderall addict, and he also helped me get my insurance to cover my stay in rehab. I feel really sad and depressed, and after a lot of thought and speaking to Dr. 7, I decide to go on an antidepressant. It is a thoughtful decision for me—I am a pill user, and I want to think through the decision to make sure it is the right one. I don't want to have the same mentality that a pill will just fix things for me. That was my thinking with Adderall, and I want to think differently about antidepressants. I make sure the medicine he prescribes is not going to make me gain weight. I have finally started making progress with my weight loss and I don't want to reverse it. I don't want to go back to fat Vitale.

I know it is probably the placebo effect, but the medicine works. I have a new outlook on life. I update my resume and send it out to my contacts in Lexington. I am ready to make the move back—and I know I want out of the legal industry. I have been working for lawyers for seven and half years and I am ready for a change. I value my quality of life in sobriety—something I did not value in active addiction.

A lot happens quickly—which is not unusual for me. Once I decide, I go into action. There is no turning back. In a matter of weeks, I celebrate one year of sobriety, decide to make a move back to Lexington, accept a new job, and turn in my notice for my current job.

* * *

I am at my office, tying up all the loose ends at the law firm. I look down at my phone and see several missed calls from my mom. Which is strange for the middle of the day—well—it is strange for any time of the day. I even have a missed text from dad that says, "Call me." I call my parents—and they answer in a rush. "Your sister has been in a terrible car accident," says my mom. "She's being airlifted to the hospital as we speak. We are headed there right now. We have Bentley with us—he's safe."

My sister could possibly die. I don't want to realize the severity of it all. It has been more than a year since I made my amends to her. Thank God I did that. Thank God I apologized for the way I treated her. I pack up my things and head to Huntsville. I arrive at the hospital and she is in critical care. My parents are there with Bentley; he has been living with them for the past few months, and Frankie's husband is there with his mom. Frankie and her husband were driving down the highway and somehow veered off the road uncontrollably in a construction zone. Frankie was driving the car, and it flipped. We couldn't get any facts about the car crash—only that Frankie had drugs in her system and her husband was in the passenger seat, but he left the scene without a scratch. Frankie is near death. Thank God Bentley wasn't in the car with them.

I walk into the waiting room of the hospital and assume the role of leader—it is unspoken—I am the one calling the shots. Always. None of us are allowed back to see her and we haven't been updated in hours—all we know is that she is in very critical condition. I play out all the scenarios in my mind—my sister dies, and Bentley must live with my parents—or he ends up living with me. I can't imagine being a parent—it's not something I think I want to do. And I definitely don't want to take on the responsibility of being Bentley's parent. How would that even work? But then again, we have this fondness for each other. I feel a closeness to him since he shares my blood and we share familial trauma.

I start thinking about how I would have to console my parents and how their daughter's death would tear them apart. My mom's drinking and drugging would end up being ten times worse than it is currently. Our worlds would be rocked.

We also need to shelter Bentley from the reality of it all. His life has been complete chaos from the day he was born—he has never lived in one place for more than a few months and my sister used him to barter for money. She would let my parents keep him in return for cash. It is insanity. She doesn't have a job, and she lives off the money my parents give her in exchange for Bentley, drug dealing, and any money her husband makes from odd jobs.

Frankie survives but barely. She has a broken pelvis, a broken collar bone, and a broken arm, and she is blind in her left eye. There were no other cars involved in the accident—Frankie is the only one harmed. How she made it, I don't know. Her injuries are severe. And after the car accident she goes crazy. She probably has untreated PTSD from the car accident. She starts using more drugs and we don't hear from her for weeks—we don't know where she is living or how she is making ends meet. When she does call, she is always angry. My parents end up getting permanent custody of Bentley.

* * *

I detach from my family drama by focusing on my move back to Lexington. I rent a basement apartment with no windows. Well, there are windows that let the light in, but I can't see the sky or the air. I start my new job and I love it. I go to some meetings and get a new sponsor, but my life revolves around exercise and a strict diet. I am determined to lose the weight and it is my new drug. My life is out of control—my family is in total chaos mode, Tom and I are hanging on by a thread, I have taken a significant pay cut at my new job, I don't know if it is the right move for me, and I am struggling to find my place—I don't know how to make my new life fit into my old life. I am having a complete identity crisis. Controlling my exercise and what I put in my mouth are my refuges. I am obsessed. It is my new drug. I have replaced Adderall with diet and exercise.

ELEVEN

A New Addiction

I'm staring at the clock. It's 3:50 p.m. If I can sneak out of work by 4:00 p.m., I can make it to my workout class at 4:30 p.m., and then get home to shower in time for dinner with the girls. I still need to Google the menu to make sure there's something I can eat, or at least modify, on the menu. That's my life—work, exercise, and eating protein, veggies, and some fruits. I never miss a workout. To miss a workout means I could gain weight. I can't do that. And then there's dinner with the girls. I need to control my weight so I can be perfect and control how I feel. To be skinny means I will feel good. But it's never good enough. Never. I'm 121 pounds now and that seems heavy. My goal weight used to be 130, but now it's 118. I need to weigh 118 pounds. When I weighed myself first thing this morning, I weighed 121—at least I haven't gained any weight.

The clock turns to 4:00 p.m. and I quietly leave the office. No one will notice if I'm gone. I've been here since 7:00 a.m. anyway, and all my work is done. I need to exercise, but I can't fit it in until 4:30 p.m. I also don't want to get in trouble for leaving work early. This is a daily battle for me. Leaving work early and then feeling guilty about it.

I get to my gym and run to change into my clothes. It's a group exercise class—I need to get a treadmill spot so I can burn more calories. If I don't get a treadmill spot, then I'll have to start with weights and I'll never get my heart rate high enough and I won't burn enough calories. I look around at all the other women waiting in line for class. The woman with the designer workout clothes has the perfect body—she's so thin. If only I could be that thin. The fact that I weighed 121 pounds this morning doesn't even register. When I look in the mirror, I see someone who weighs 180 pounds, not 121. My clothing size can't even convince me I'm skinny.

It's probably a fluke or wrong or mismarked. It can't be right. I can't be wearing a size twenty-six or a two. I wasn't even this thin on Adderall—well, maybe I was once—like in 2008. But it doesn't matter—it's not good enough. I want to lose more.

All the other women have beautiful bodies. I wish I could just be happy with my body. I stare at my reflection in the glass door and all I see are hips, big hips. Ugh. I just want to be happy. I'm never enough. And it's never good enough. I feel unworthy and overweight, and it consumes me. I will do anything—outside of drugs and alcohol—to feel perfect. Class starts and I get a treadmill spot. Thank God. It's a high intensity workout and I push myself hard—and I do this every day. And the days I can't make it to class, I go for a five- or seven-mile run. I must get a workout in every single day. If I skip, I chance gaining weight. And I don't want to feel that way. I can't handle that feeling.

I rush home from the workout to get in the shower and get ready for dinner with my girlfriends. We haven't seen one another in forever. They are a big reason for my moving back. They are the people in my life that are healthy for me. They are my chosen family, who support my sobriety and don't push me to do things I don't want to do. I can't wait to see them, but I don't know what I'm going to eat. And I'm starving. I put a few pieces of gum in my mouth to tie me over. That will do. I get out of the shower and avoid my reflection in the mirror. I don't want to look at myself—it's too much. I put on the same pair of jeans and an extra-small sweater that I normally wear out—I don't have many other choices because everything else in my closet is too big. Nothing fits. But it doesn't matter—I won't stay this size for long. I will gain weight. I always do. I don't trust my body.

I rush to dinner and I'm the first to arrive. I can finally breathe. But I'm in my head. What am I going to eat? I'm starving. What are my friends going to think? When am I going to exercise tomorrow? I'm wondering if the half avocado in my salad today had too many calories. Maybe I will gain weight. My friends arrive a few minutes later and I'm excited to see them, but I'm worn out. My workout today was hard, and I don't eat carbs anymore, so there's that. I need to eat right now. I'm irritable. My friends are talking, but I just want to order. I signal to our server that we are ready.

I don't know if everyone else has had time to look at the menu, but I don't care. I'm starving. I order fish without the sauce and no potatoes and extra veggies. That's always what I do. I need to control what I eat. My friends pass the breadbasket around the table and it misses me. Bread is too scary to eat. If I eat it, I may never be able to stop eating it.

Moderation has never been my strength. I cut things out entirely—it has been one year since I've had any sweets or carbs, and I'm not drinking alcohol, which has been a saving grace since it's so high in sugar. Seriously—a whole damn year. But I don't miss any of these things, and if I tried just one, I wouldn't be able to stop myself. I would binge.

This drug of choice—of not eating and overexercising—is at least legal. It feels much less secretive. All my friends know I'm trying to lose the weight I gained in early sobriety. Except I've already lost it. I've lost more weight with this addiction than I ever did with Adderall. And while I feel shame, I also feel good. I'm the thinnest of all my friends. I'm the fittest and I can run the fastest mile. I'm committed to my "health." It's this crazy paradox—I'm the thinnest I've ever been and yet it's not enough. Every time I reach my goal weight, I change my goal weight so I can lose more. It's never enough. And when I look in the mirror, I don't see someone who weighs 121 pounds, I see someone who weighs 180 pounds. And yet, I know it's insane. It's crazy to intellectually know I'm thin, but emotionally I feel fat.

* * *

I walk into my Dr. 7's office. I see him every Tuesday at 1:00 p.m. He's been with me since before rehab, so he really knows me. He knows me as a drug-seeking addict, and he knows me as a recovering addict. Our sessions are focused on my weight or my unhealthy relationship with Tom or my mom's most recent relapse or the latest family drama. I'm either complaining about Tom and how I want out of the relationship, or I'm talking about my current weight. It's so surface level. I walk into the waiting area and push the button with his name on it to signal that I'm here for my session. While I'm waiting, I start reflecting on what it used to be like for me in this waiting room. Not that long ago, I was here drug seeking. I was here hoping and praying he would write me an Adderall prescription. I would anxiously wait for him in hopes of getting my next high—in hopes of getting my promise of perfection.

Dr. 7 opens the door to get me for our session, and my thoughts of the past are interrupted. This is my reality now—I'm sober and weight obsessed and unhappier than ever. I don't want to admit it, but I'm fucking unhappy. I sit down on the edge of his leather sofa—I don't want to get too comfortable and relaxed. He asks me how I'm doing, and I'm quiet. I don't have anything that I want to talk about. "Well, I got on the scale this morning and I weigh 117 pounds. Yesterday I was 116 pounds. But today I weigh more. And I feel fat and ugly," I say. He looks shocked by my weight admission. He knows my weight—I see him every week and it's all I can talk about. But today, he reacts differently. "You need to get your bloodwork done. I want to make sure your potassium levels are okay. I will write you a prescription to get that done this week," he responds. What is he even talking about? That sounds serious. Why is he so concerned?

"Why do you want me to do that?" I ask.

"I'm concerned about your weight and I want to make sure you are at normal potassium levels," he says, and then he pauses. "Have you ever considered that you have an eating disorder?" I don't know how to respond. I'm in shock. An eating disorder? That sounds a little extreme. It's not like I'm in the hospital or anything. I feel totally fine. I feel healthy, I guess. I mean—why would he say that? "That sounds a bit extreme," I reply. "I don't have an eating disorder."

He looks at me and I can tell he's waiting for me to come to my own conclusion that I have an eating disorder. But I'm not having it. To admit I have an eating disorder makes me a victim. I'm done playing the victim. I was a slave to Adderall and now I'm sober. So that means I'm healthy, right? He then goes on to explain that there are varying degrees of eating disorders—just like there are varying degrees of addictions. He says that an eating disorder is basically an unhealthy relationship with food. It can be eating too much or too little, bingeing or purging or restricting. There's not one type of eating disorder.

I'm flooded with emotion, and I break down in heavy tears, sobbing.

I cover my face with both of my hands as if I don't want him or anyone else to know I'm crying. "How can this be true?" I say over my tears. I can hardly say the words. To admit I have an eating disorder is something I'm just not ready to do. "Vitale, you have an eating disorder," he says. Fuck. Fuck. Fuck. Fine—I'll be open-minded. Maybe I have an eating disorder, but not a bad one. Not the kind of eating disorder you see on a Lifetime television movie.

I calm down from my intense crying episode, and I wipe the tears from my face. Thank goodness I didn't wear mascara today. That would be a disaster—then everyone would know I was crying. "Okay, so let's say I have an eating disorder," I say. "What does that mean?" He just looks at me and gives me time to think. I'm trying to process this information that was just dropped on me. I might have an eating disorder. If an eating disorder is any unhealthy relationship with food, then I probably have one. I have an unhealthy relationship with food—I've cut out most food groups. I only eat protein and veggies. I obsess about what I eat, and if I eat anything outside my food rules, I immediately feel guilt and shame. Fuck. I have an eating disorder. I'm sure he's fully entertained by the fact that I've come out of complete denial about my eating disorder in this session. He's probably giving himself a high-five for a job well done. It's more than I can bear.

My tears and sadness turn to anger. In the span of thirty minutes, I've gone from not having an eating disorder to possibly having an eating disorder, to having an eating disorder, and then to feeling sad about it, to feeling anger. I've evolved a lot over the past thirty minutes. And now I'm angry. I'm not sad—I'm fucking angry. How can I have a fucking eating disorder? I just spent the past ten years of my life addicted to Adderall, and now I have an eating disorder. Are you kidding me? How did I get here? How is this even possible? My anger has turned into rage. I thought I had cured my addiction—I was no longer taking Adderall or drinking. But I guess there's more to it.

How did I let this happen? I thought I was done with my addiction. But I'm not done—it's manifested itself into disordered eating. I say it out loud, "Okay. I guess I have an eating disorder." He looks at me and smiles,

"Yes, you do, Vitale. You have an eating disorder." For some reason it feels good to have another person validate me.

"So, our time is up for today," he says.

"Okay—thank you," I say. "But what do I do now? What do I do with my eating disorder?"

"Just take some time between sessions to think about it and accept it. And go get your bloodwork done," he responds. I take the prescription for my bloodwork, and I get up and walk out. The range of emotion I just experienced has worn me out. I'm enlightened, I'm overwhelmed, I'm angry, and I'm sad. I'm sad that I'm dealing with this. I'm ready for my addiction to be over. I'm ready to live my life.

A few months pass, and I'm now using my eating disorder as an excuse to have an eating disorder. I'm down to 112 pounds. Everyone around me is worried. My friends are worried. Tom is worried—although he plays along with my dysfunction. I'm controlling about what I eat and when I exercise, and he doesn't ask questions. We are so disconnected anyway that it doesn't matter. I don't want to be with him, but I don't know how to leave. I don't want to be alone, but I'm miserable. We spend time together, but we're not connected. We've only had sex a dozen times in the past year and it's because I have zero sex drive. And I have zero interest in our relationship. I'm disconnected mentally. We've been through so much together at this point—affair, divorce, sobriety—we must be meant to be, right? I don't know. I'm comfortably miserable. But at least it's a known misery. It's a misery that's familiar to me. I don't want to think about it because I'm not ready to deal with it.

At least now I can admit I have a problem. I go over to my friend's house for dinner and they serve food that's outside my food rules, and I politely decline—"it's my eating disorder." It's ridiculous. I want to get better, but I don't. And what would it mean to start eating normally and gaining weight? How would I feel? I'm not ready to dip my toes in those waters yet. I'm just ready to admit I have a problem—I'm not ready to deal with it yet.

My eating disorder is my priority. What I eat, when I exercise, and what I weigh dictate my life. And although it can be sad, it's also feels good to fit into a size twenty-five jean. I mean a size twenty-five—I don't think I've ever been this thin. And I did it without Adderall. How could I get this thin without my Adderall? It seems impossible, but it's not. It's completely possible. And to control my weight means I control how I feel. And the less I weigh, the better I feel. The more perfect I am. But not really. The less I weigh, the less I feel. The less space I take up. The less I have to deal with my underlying emotions. Being thin and controlling my weight is a Band-Aid for my pain and my past and my trauma. And once I remove that Band-Aid, there's no going back. I'll have to face it.

I need to buy new clothes because nothing fits me. I walk into a store—and I pick up a few pairs of pants and skirts in size two and four—this should fit me. I go back to the dressing room and I take my clothes off. I see my reflection in the mirror. I look away and I try on the size four first—I don't want to be disappointed if the size two doesn't fit. The size four is hanging off me. I try on the size two and it does the same thing. I can't believe I'm too small for a size two—what is wrong with me? I feel so much shame. I ask one of the store associates to give me a few size zeros—I can't believe I'm even asking that—I sound pretentious. Doesn't everyone want to be a size zero? Not me—not if it feels this way. The size zero is still too big—but there's nothing smaller. I feel sick to my stomach—I can't even fit into the smallest size—I guess I will just pin it.

* * *

It's November, and I've been sober from Adderall and alcohol for almost a year and a half now. It's Tom's birthday weekend and I planned a weekend in Nashville. I haven't been the best girlfriend, so it's time to redeem myself. I haven't been giving him much attention or showing him enough love, so maybe this gesture will make up for all my other missteps. Maybe it will make up for my absence. I don't want to do it, but I feel like I should do it. We spend the weekend shopping and eating at the best restaurants in Nashville. I spend my time obsessing over what to eat, while Tom eats and drinks whatever he wants. His drinking bothers me, but I push it down because I don't feel like dealing with it. We exercise twice while we're there because I never miss a workout. After the second workout, I get on the scale—because that's what I do. It reads 103 pounds. Holy shit. One hundred and three pounds. How did I lose that much weight? How did I get this small? The scale must be broken. There's no way I weigh 103 pounds. I don't know what to think or do or say. I hop off the scale. I wait for it to clear and hop on again—I need to be sure it isn't a mistake. And sure enough—it reads 103 pounds again. I get off the scale the second time and get fully dressed. I'm in complete disbelief. I don't think I look this thin—or do I? Do I look this skinny? My arms are rail thin, which is why I never wear sleeveless tops to the gym anymore—but how does that translate into 103 pounds? There's no fucking way. I step outside the gym and Tom is waiting for me on the bench outside.

"I just weighed myself in there," I say to him. "And the scale says I weigh 103 pounds. How is that possible? That can't be correct?" Tom doesn't even respond to my comment. He changes the subject and we move on throughout our day. Except I don't. I'm in complete disbelief about my weight. I feel so much shame. I know I had lost more weight, but I didn't realize it was this much. I know none of my clothes fit, but I didn't realize the seriousness of it all. I didn't realize it had gotten this bad. How did I not know? Everyone around me is concerned but I didn't get it. Until now.

We get home from the weekend and I fall into a deep sadness. I desperately want to change, but I don't know how to start. I need to fix this—and I start looking at everything outside myself first. I'm not ready to deal with my eating and weight just yet—maybe I can chip away at other things that are making me unhappy. Like my relationship. That's a major source of unhappiness and unfulfillment. Maybe if I end that I will feel better? I start disconnecting from Tom even more than before. Everything he does or doesn't do bothers me—his drinking, his age, his air of superiority, our inability to communicate and connect, his resentment and anger toward me. We are cold and out of touch with each other. There is no love between us. And I can't ignore it anymore. I'm on a mission to deal with it—but not yet.

It's December and I want to end things with Tom, but it's the holidays. It's Christmas—who ends their relationship during the holidays? The holidays are already so lonely for me anyway and I'm not sure I want to be lonelier. I'm not sure I can handle it. But there's a void in our relationship and I can't ignore it any longer. We are hardly communicating—we are merely existing. We are on autopilot in our relationship—it's unhealthy and neither of us want to pull the trigger on it. Tom will never end it, so I will have to do it. He pretends like everything is okay—and it isn't. How can he think this is okay? How can he think it's okay to be in the same room and never talk? I always wanted to build my life with someone—and we aren't building anything but walls between us. High walls made of stone. And there's no getting through.

I'm at a spin class on New Year's Day and I can't take it anymore. It's an all-female class and the instructor is playing music that speaks to my soul. She says to the class that instead of adding things to your list of New Year's resolutions, what if we resolved to remove things from our list? Like toxic people, places, or things from our lives. This message is made for me. Maybe I need to remove toxicity from my life. I keep pedaling and I start crying. Thank God the room is dark so no one can see me. I cannot escape this message. I cannot hide from the truth any longer. I need to end it with Tom, and I need to do it today. I get home from spin and I shower and head over to Tom's. I tell him we need to talk. He's used to these cryptic messages from me, but he will be blindsided by the breakup. He shouldn't be blindsided because we are both deeply unhappy—well—I'm deeply unhappy—I'm not sure about him. He's probably in denial and drinking his way through life. But it's a deeply unhealthy and unfixable relationship.

I pull into his driveway and I park my car. I take a deep breath. This is the right thing to do. I can do this. I text Meghan and tell her I'm about to break up with Tom, and that I will call her afterward. I'm ready to end things. I need to do this. I cannot ignore my pain and unhappiness any longer. I walk into his house and he's making a martini—of course he is. It's 2:00 p.m. on New Year's Day—why not? His drinking just reconfirms my decision. I can do this, I tell myself. I sit down on one of his barstools in the kitchen. I have zero feeling or emotion on my face. If I get emotional, then I won't be able to do it. I won't be able to end it. Plus, he might talk me out of it. I've talked about ending it before and he was able to sweet talk me out of it and had me questioning my own thoughts and decisions.

That's the one thing with Tom, I never trust myself when I'm around him. He always acts like he knows me better than I know myself. And I'm done with that bullshit. I know what I want. I know myself. I look him in the eyes and I quickly cut to the chase. There's no sugar coating anything with me. I need to deal with it now and I need to deal with it directly. I have zero feeling in my eyes or tone of voice. I do that to protect myself. "Tom, this isn't working anymore," I say. "I'm really unhappy, and you're unhappy. I don't want to be with you anymore."

He looks at me completely calmly. "Are you serious, Vitale?" he responds. "You've got to be kidding me. You're going to come over here and unilaterally make decisions that impact both of us. After everything we've been through?" His tone of voice gets more aggressive and I start feeling guilty. But I had anticipated that. I had anticipated that he would want to make me feel this way. I need to stay strong. I need to follow through. He wants a full explanation as to why I want out of the relationship, but I don't have one. All I know is that I'm deeply unhappy. And even though I tell him that, it's not enough. I can't point to one thing in particular—it's all of it. I'm no longer physically or emotionally attracted to him. I could say that, but it would be too hurtful. Too honest. I look at him with no emotion or feeling and I tell him it's over. He responds with, "Okay Vitale. If that's what you want." It is what I want. I know that if I stay any longer, I will change my mind. So I leave. I've broken up with him before but never as a sober person. It's different this time. I mean it. I get into my car and I drive off.

* * *

I gain seven pounds over the next six weeks, so I'm at 110 or 111 pounds. It's not ideal, but it's better than 103 pounds. I'm still obsessing, but I've been working with a nutritionist to introduce new foods into my diet and rewrite my food rules—or maybe better said, eliminating my food rules. Which I'm not quite ready to do, but I'm making progress.

Spending time with my best friends over the past few days has been soul giving. Meghan has been talking about getting a cat, so we stop by the local pet store to see if we can find one for her. I've never considered getting a pet. In fact, it's something my friends find strange about me. But it makes sense—I've been very self-focused for most of my life, and an animal would totally cramp my style. We go back to look at the dogs and my friends start saying I should get a dog. I guess they think it would be good for me—that I could use a companion. It sounds crazy, but it kind of feels right.

I look at the dogs in their cages. They seem sad. None of them speak to me, until I walk back to the very last cage—there's a black and white speckled mutt named Corman. He moves toward me in his cage and our noses touch. I can't move away; there's something pulling me. I ask one of the employees to let me hold him and play with him. And I'm immediately hooked. Immediately. He is my dog. But this is crazy. How can I take care of a dog? I've never been responsible for anything other than myself and that's been more than I can handle. But it feels right. And he feels like my soul dog. He picked me.

Becoming a dog owner is a significant event in my life. It's significant because for the first time in my life I shift the focus off me onto Corman—onto something other than myself. For the first time in my life, I am responsible for something other than myself. Corman begins to shine a light in dark corners of my life. He helps crack me open.

Focusing on Corman distracts me from my weight obsession. I still exercise every day, but I am introducing new foods into my diet. I start adding yogurt and oatmeal and fruit and cheese. And it isn't easy to do this, but I know I have to do something different if I want to shake my new addiction. I know I need to change, and that means I have to challenge my current way of living. I can no longer just focus on me, me, and me. Corman gives me a reason to change. He helps me see that life is bigger than me. He starts my process of true healing. I start to gain weight in a healthy way—I am finally back to 121 pounds.

The weight gain isn't only about eating, it is about dealing with the shame that I began to uncover back at the treatment center. Why would I want my body to disappear? Why would the pain be vibrating through my bones, an emotional pain that manifested in a circulation of self-hatred? I keep journaling about my lack of comfort in my body. I have only once thought about possibly being molested. It is time for me to heal myself once and for all.

My Aunt Catheryn has always been a close friend to me. I trust her in ways I can't trust my own mother. I think she could be my memory of sorts, or at least let me know if I am completely crazy for thinking this in the first place.

"I have something I need to ask you," I say with trepidation. "This is an odd question, but I just need to ask it." There is a slight pause on the other line. I don't even wait for her to respond. "Um—do you know if I was molested when I was child?" There is silence on the other end.

"Well," she says. "I know that when you were three years old, you accused one of the ladies at your day care of touching you, and she ended up being fired." My heart stops. I was molested. By a woman.

My aunt then goes on to explain that after it happened, I wouldn't let people touch me or bathe me, and I wouldn't walk around without panties on. And I was only three. At three years old, I was already ashamed of my body. At three years old, I knew something had happened—and I knew it was wrong, and I used body shame for survival.

My story unfolds in front of me like a game of dominoes, where one domino impacts all the other dominoes. This is my first domino. This domino impacts my entire life—the chips are all falling into place. This domino impacts how I see myself in the mirror, how I relate to the opposite sex, how my clothes fit me, whether I feel comfortable going out with friends because of my body weight, my deep desire to be perfect, how I talk to myself, how I allow myself to be touched—I mean this is the seedling domino. All the pieces of my life start making sense. I feel validation and worthiness and I feel seen. For the first time, I feel seen. I feel understood—or rather, maybe for the first time I understand myself. I know why I am the way I am—and I can change it. I can't change the past, but I can change who I am moving forward. I can learn to let go and heal my body shame. I can learn to let go of my deeply rooted body hate.

I can stop punishing my body for something out of my control. I can stop the dieting and the exercise obsession and the food obsession. I can stop it. And I can move on.

I hang up my phone and text Dr. 7 to see if he has any available appointments this week. My body is 100 percent certain of the truth—but my brain is trying to talk me out of it. "You're making this a bigger deal than it needs to be, Vitale," I think to myself. "Stop trying to make something out of nothing. Leave the past in the past. Stop being so dramatic."

A few days later, I walk into Dr.7's office—he knows my life in intimate detail—he will understand. He will be able to help me make sense of this. He will see that my eating disorder is tied to this as well. He will help me understand the next steps in my journey.

I sit on his leather couch. I have never liked this couch. Sometimes I sit on the very edge of the couch, and other times I sit all the way back, relaxed—it just depends on the subject matter of the session. This time I sit on the edge.

"Okay—so I discovered something about my childhood, and so much about me makes sense now," I say. I start telling him what I discovered—I am so excited to tell him—it feels like all the puzzle pieces of my life fit together finally. Finally. And now it can make sense to him.

"Well," he says, "I'm not sure that happened to you, Vitale. You don't exhibit any signs of someone who has been sexually abused. If you can't remember it, I don't think it happened to you. You may be making something out of nothing."

I am dumbfounded. What about my promiscuity, my need to avoid and numb, my eating disorder that he diagnosed me with, the codependency and need for approval, the discomfort with touch and intimacy? How could he say this? How could he minimize my experience? He doesn't know me—he doesn't know what happened to me. I start questioning myself and my experience. I start giving my power away to him—like he knows me better than I know myself.

We finish the session, and I walk out of his office, like a ghost. My body is once again separate from my soul. My world is crashing down on me—I can't separate fact from fiction. It is like my childhood—when

I knew something to be true and then some adult would swoop in and tear it all apart—telling me that what I know isn't true. It is like when I know my mom is drunk and she denies, denies, denies. And even though I know for a fact she has been drinking, her denial causes me to be in denial—maybe I am wrong? Maybe she's not drunk? Maybe she's just tired or sick or angry? Maybe I'm wrong. She knows better than me. For so much of my life I have allowed other people to know me better than me. I allowed other people to define my human experience. It was learned from my childhood. I would know my mom was drinking and then my dad would cover for her and tell me I was wrong. And that's when I started questioning myself. Or it probably started when I was three and I was molested by my daycare teacher—I spoke my truth, and everyone questioned me. I've been giving away my power since I was three years old. It isn't going to be easy to unlearn this—but it's going to be worth it. This is the beginning of a major shift in my life. This is the beginning of me taking my power back.

TWELVE
Breakthrough

My grandmother turns ninety this year, and I want to spend more time with her. We have grown distant during my addiction and in my relationship with Tom. She used to be my best friend—we talked at least once a day, and now we talk once a week, at best. I want to rebuild my relationship with her while she is still alive. And this is something new to me—focusing on someone other than myself. My addiction—both Adderall and food and exercise—was all about me and my needs. I didn't give a fuck about anyone else. But that isn't me anymore and I don't want to live like that. I want to change. I want to let love back into my life.

In the background of my healing are my family's drama and chaos. My parents now have permanent custody of Bentley and he is four years old. My mom is basically raising him by herself because my dad travels each week. I try not to get involved because I need boundaries and it is too much for me emotionally. I am either all in or all out, and it is easier for me to be all out. But something deep inside me knows that my nephew deserves more. His life has been filled with trauma and chaos and misfortune, and although he is in a better place with my parents—it is still unhealthy. My mom is still drinking and taking Xanax and that means Bentley is having a childhood parallel to mine. He is being raised by people who are hurting and unhealed. And God knows how that played out for me. I've been in therapy for three years and counting. And I still have years of work to do to unlearn the patterns and trauma from my childhood. I don't know what the solution is for Bentley, but I know something has to change. And the crazy thing is I am not even emotionally attached to Bentley. I fell in love with him the day he was born, but I didn't allow myself to get close to him because it hurt too much. To be close to him means I would be too close to my family drama. I keep my distance—both physically and emotionally. But something is tugging at my heart.

I visit my grandmother in St. Louis for the second time this year. I vow to spend more time with family, and I am following through on my commitments. I arrive and my grandmother immediately criticizes my weight. "You're too thin, Vitale," she said. "Eat something. You look unhealthy." She can never keep her mouth closed about anything—which is something I inherited from her. She and I are very similar—we are both left-handed, strong willed, smart, determined, and unwavering. She taught me how to be a strong woman. She taught me to be disciplined and strong. But you know what they say about similar people; they tend to butt heads occasionally. During my Adderall addiction, I would spend time with my grandmother and aunt, but I was never present. I never allowed myself to enjoy the moment because I was already onto the next moment. Plus, I was only concerned with my own wants and needs. I would visit, but I wasn't visiting. I was there physically, but I kept to my own schedule. I would go shopping or smoke cigarettes and drink. I would do the bare minimum to make myself feel like a good grandchild and niece. And then in my exercise addiction, I was a little better, but not much. Instead of shopping and smoking and drinking, I was exercising and obsessing about what I put in my mouth. But this visit is different. I am present and connected. I am more focused on how I can help versus what I can get. My priorities and needs are on the back burner. For the first time, I show up to serve and be present and engage. I spend the last night at home with my Aunt Catheryn and my grandmother, which is unusual because my aunt and uncle own a restaurant and Saturday nights are busy. But the three of us spend quality time together—for the first time in my adult life. We are going through old pictures and eating dinner together. I haven't been this close to my aunt since I was a kid, and it is nice to spend quality time with them. The timing of everything is uncanny.

The three of us start talking about my mom and Bentley and the chaos at home. We talk about how Bentley is not safe with my mom because her drinking is still out of control. And it is. My parents have been Bentley's primary guardians for the past six months. During this time, my sister has stopped by only two or three times to visit her son. The accident changed her—it made her more needy and so she prioritizes her husband over her son. Her drug use escalated, and we don't know where she is living—or if she is living. She has several warrants out for her arrest. It is the perfect storm. And then there is poor little Bentley—defenseless and yearning for love. The love that I yearned for when I was younger—and to some degree even now I yearn for.

I'm not certain what has gotten into me, but I feel safe with my aunt and my grandmother. Something shifts in me. I feel present and calm and connected. In the middle of our conversation, I blurt out, "What if I adopt Bentley?" I can't believe that those words come out of my mouth. My chest grows tight. What would they think? How would they respond? I am a recovering drug addict—what do I know about raising a child? Well, I know a lot since I basically raised myself. My aunt looks at my grandmother and they both smile. I don't know why. Are they going to laugh at me?

"We've been waiting for you to say that for a long time, Vitale," says my aunt. "Really?" I respond.

"Yes, we've been thinking you would be the best person to raise Bentley, but that's not something you can tell someone to do. It's something you have to decide for yourself because it's such a serious commitment," she says. I feel relieved and honored and validated. Maybe I can do this? I don't know how I'm going to do this or how it is going to happen, but if my aunt and grandmother believe in me, then I can do this. I will never forget this day. It was April 22, 2016.

The three of us begin brainstorming ways to bring this idea to my parents. It can't be about my mom's drinking because my mom and dad would get too defensive. We have to make it about my parent's age—they need to be grandparents, not parents. I am young and capable of raising him. They are in their sixties and they don't need to play mom and dad to a four-year-old. They need to be grandparents. And Bentley deserves a healthy and safe and consistent home environment. And that's something I can provide for him. Being a parent is never something I aspired to be, but something is calling me to do this. Something way bigger and greater than myself. I need to figure out the best way to sell this to my parents. And I pray and pray about it.

* * *

I make it back to Lexington and I wonder what my friends will think about this idea. They will probably think I am crazy. I call my friends and my sponsor to see what they think about it, and to my surprise, everyone is fully supportive. They are shocked—but they are supportive. Everyone believes in me. And it's taking everyone's belief in me to pursue this—because I am having a hard time believing in me—this is so far outside any of my life plans. Of course, so is everything that has happened in my life.

I pray and pray. I know I need to turn to God for this. This decision is way bigger than me. There is a child involved and that means I need to hand it over to God and let go—which isn't a strength of mine—control is my strength. The biggest blessing in all this is that I completely let go of the outcome. I mean—completely. I hand the outcome over to God. I take action, but I know that whatever is in Bentley's best interest will happen. Whether that is with me, or my sister, or my parents—that is up to God. And thank God I am able to do that.

A few days pass and I decide to put my idea out there. I pray about it and I am as ready as I will ever be. I practice what I will say to my parents when I call them. "Mom and Dad—there's something important I want to talk about with you." I rehearse the conversation in my head. I say another prayer, take a deep breath, and dial their number. My dad answers the phone. "Dad, I would like to talk with you and mom about something important," I say firmly. I'm sure they are wondering what I am going to say or ask. I never give people a warning—I just call them or sit them down and deal with it directly. I'm sure there's a softer way of dealing with things, but this is my way. At least for now. I want to deal with it and move on.

"Yes," says my dad. I ask if he can put me on speaker so I can talk with him and mom at the same time. I want to get their reaction together.

"Mom, Dad," I pause. "I've been thinking and praying about something that I want you to really consider. I would like for you all to consider letting me be Bentley's parent, so y'all can be grandparents." There is silence on the other line. I don't know how they will react. I don't know how I will react. The silence continues. A million thoughts race through my mind—what are they thinking? Am I sure I want to do this? Will my mom know this is about her alcoholism? Will my dad know? The silence seems to last forever. And to be fair to them, this conversation came out of nowhere.

My dad finally breaks the silence. "Raising a child is a huge responsibility, Vitale," he says. "I don't think you understand everything that goes into it. And it would be a lifelong commitment, not something you can try on for a few months and then change your mind." I understand what he is saying, but I also know I will never be ready to be a parent. I am being divinely called to do this. It is out of my hands. It is a force bigger than me. And—at least I'm sober. I can provide him a consistent, stable, and safe home life. That's something my parents can't give him. And Bentley deserves a healthy home. He didn't ask to be brought into this world. I allow my parents to talk and I just listen. I know this is something I can't boss my way around. It will need to be carefully navigated. They tell me they need to talk and think about it. I tell them I am committed. I know this will require an in-person conversation, so I decide to visit them the following weekend to discuss it in person. I need them to understand that I am serious about this.

It is Derby weekend, and I am going home to talk to my parents. I want them to know how serious I am about Bentley. It's a big deal for a Kentuckian to miss the Derby, so I am not messing around. I pack my bags and drive the five hours to my home in Alabama. I want my parents to see I've weighed this heavily, and want to get started on spending time with Bentley. It will be a small taste of what I will be getting myself into. Well, I will never know what I am getting myself into. I bring Corman with me because I think he and Bentley will bond, which would be helpful—animals always assist in healthy interactions.

It's interesting to step back and think about all this. I have no connection to Bentley—I haven't allowed myself to get too close to him—it hurts too much. It must have been unhealed trauma from my childhood or my ego trying to protect me. But I am ready to begin the healing, and the only thing driving me to do this is a force way bigger than me.

I walk into my parent's house and they are standing in the kitchen. Bentley is on the couch in the living room watching TV. He hears me walk into the house and he turns around and smiles. Our souls are connected. I hug my parents—I'm genuinely happy to see them and scared at the same time. My mom is sober today. Thank God. There's no way I could have this conversation if she was drunk. "Want to go outside and talk?" I ask. We need to have this conversation away from Bentley—outside on the back porch seems like the best place to go. The three of us step outside. My parents sit down and they each light their cigarette. They are chain smokers—there's no escaping it. I remain standing; there's too much energy running through my body for me to sit down and I want to portray a position of strength and confidence—and standing does that better than sitting.

"I'm serious about this," I start off. "I've been praying about this and thinking about this a lot and I want to be Bentley's guardian. Forever." I can't let them know that this idea came out of my conversation with my aunt and grandmother—it's like blaming this on my mom's alcoholism—I will get nowhere. I'm not manipulating the situation; I'm just eliminating any unnecessary hurdles. And my mom's addiction and my aunt are hurdles—big ones. My dad reinforces the fact that this is a permanent decision—one that I can't change in a few months. That parenting is difficult, that I have no clue what I'm getting into, that it's a huge responsibility. I get all those things. And I can conceptually understand them, but I will never fully understand until I'm doing it. It's like any parent—no one knows what they're getting into until they get into it. And even then, they still don't know.

My mom is crying—her emotional attachment to Bentley transcends the typical grandparent-grandchild relationship. She has taken on the role of parent, somewhat out of necessity. To allow me to become the guardian would be like losing a child for her—her codependence with Bentley reminds me of her codependence with me when I was a child. It wasn't healthy then and it's not healthy now. And that's why I'm doing this—Bentley deserves a different childhood than me. I'm mission driven. My heart is guiding me through all of this.

We go back and forth all night about this and my parents finally agree. I can't believe it. But I'm grateful. My parents suggest I spend the next day with Bentley to test-drive this parenting thing, which is funny to me. Test-driving parenting—is that even a thing? Good or bad, I'm doing this. There's no turning back. My parents make one other suggestion: they've been taking Bentley to see a counselor because of all the trauma and change he's experienced. I'm proud of my parents for providing him with that. My mom thinks it's a good idea for me to meet with his counselor so she can make a recommendation on how best to move forward. I think it's a great idea. I spend the next day with Bentley—we go to the zoo, grab lunch, have sweet conversations, and eat ice cream. Ice cream is a big deal for me because of my disordered eating, but becoming a parent is much bigger than ice cream. And it's just this once.

* * *

I drive back to Lexington and everything starts falling into place. I create a mental checklist of things that need to happen to become his guardian: I need to meet with Bentley's counselor. I need to find a home to buy because my basement apartment won't cut it. I need to meet with my sponsor more frequently. I need to research schools for him to attend. And I need to look into the legal process of getting temporary guardianship—permanent guardianship will happen later. So many things need to happen. I'm excited and nervous, but it all feels right.

My parents' lawyer puts together a few documents for us to sign, granting me temporary guardianship. This takes much less time than I thought it would. I guess it is permanent guardianship that's more intensive. Temporary guardianship lasts for one year; I will figure everything else out later. I feel a sense of pride for doing this. I mean—this is a big deal. I'm becoming a parent. Holy shit.

I work down my checklist of things to do—I buy a house, I find a school that I think is best for Bentley, I've been granted temporary guardianship. All the big things are done. Now it's the emotional things that need to be handled: telling my sister, making sure everything is explained thoughtfully to Bentley, managing my parent's emotions about granting me temporary guardianship, and the reality for me that life is about to drastically change forever. I've spent thirty-three years doing whatever I want, whenever I want—and this is going to be life-changing. I have Corman; that's sort of like an introduction to parenthood. It gets me thinking about something other than myself.

I've been on autopilot, and I haven't taken the time to let everything sink in. I'm going to be responsible for a five-year-old. I will be responsible for his emotional and physical well-being. I need to make sure he has friends. I need to make sure he's learning the right things. I need to make sure I model the right behavior. I need to make sure I do it differently than my parents. I need to make sure I set aside time for me—God knows I'm an introvert at heart. I can't believe I bought a house and that I'm doing this. I've never made this type of commitment in my life. In fact, Bentley is the first time I've fully committed to anything. Even in my long-term relationships, I was never fully committed. And this time, I am all in.

Moving day arrives and I'm doing it all alone. I mean, I hired movers but no one else is helping me—no friends or ex-boyfriends, no family. I'm doing it all by myself, but for some reason this time it affects me. I'm used to doing things on my own; why does this seem harder? And I'm more emotional and a little needy. I'm irrationally angry that no one is helping me. I didn't ask anyone to help—but no one offered either. *It's just me. It's always just me.*

Four hours later and I'm alone in my new house on Memory Lane— the street name is sweet—I love it. There are boxes everywhere. The house is quiet, and I feel so lonely. I'm all by myself. I walk out to my back porch and sit down on the steps. The sun is setting; it will be pitch dark soon. There are fireflies lighting up my backyard. I love summertime. I can feel the tears coming on, and I start crying uncontrollably. I'm sure all my new neighbors can hear me sobbing, but I can't make it stop. I rest my elbows on my knees and I put my head in my hands. I need to feel supported. Maybe that's what I'm doing subconsciously—trying to support myself.

I have one week to get my house in order until Bentley moves in. It's the Fourth of July holiday so I have a few extra days off work to get everything completed. My friend's husband sets up Bentley's bunkbed for me, and I buy dinosaur sheets and a comforter to make him feel welcome. I'm excited about this next chapter in my life. But I'm also in shock. The house, the kid, the guardianship—it all came together in a matter of months. And it was all God. This wouldn't have happened without God.

My parents arrive on July 8, 2016—they plan on staying a few nights to help get Bentley acclimated to his new home. Bentley is scared and excited and hopeful. He just wants somewhere he can call home. He wants a family and he deserves a family. He deserves a home. And I'm giving him that. The four of us run errands all over Lexington to get things for my new house—kitchen drawer organizers and laundry detergent and a shower curtain liner—all the basics. I'm awkward around Bentley—it's like I don't know how to act as his parent—I only know how to be the fun aunt. Not the rule-making parent. But the role of parent comes easy to me because I've been a parent most of my life. I'm trying to manage my relationship with Bentley and my parents' relationship with Bentley. My mom is fragile right now—she and Bentley have a codependency on one another. It's unhealthy, but it will change over time—it will have to change. Bentley is still calling me Aunt Lolly, and my mom corrects him, "It's not Aunt Lolly anymore; it's Mom." I appreciate what she's doing, but it feels strange. I don't want to force him to call me anything he's not comfortable with. He's already been yanked from place to place to place— he's experienced more trauma and change in his five years of life than most adults. He's a sweet innocent boy. And thank God for Corman—the bond between a boy and his dog is special. At least Bentley and Corman can be best friends—it's stability for Bentley. And Corman can sense that Bentley needs love and attention, which is exactly what he gives him. He follows Bentley around like a bodyguard.

That evening my Aunt Catheryn calls to tell us that my grandmother is not doing well—she might not make it through the night. So much change all at once. My grandfather died the year before, and now it is my grandmother. She made it to her ninetieth birthday, but she is done holding on. Hospice has been at her house for a few weeks, so we know it could be any day—but it never registers until it happens. My mom and dad go ahead and leave to spend the last few days or hours with my grandmother. I don't know whether Bentley and I should go, but everyone tells us to stay in Lexington—that's what she would have wanted. It would be too much confusion for Bentley.

* * *

I wake up the next day on July 9, 2016—it's my first day alone with Bentley. It's my first official day as a parent. I walk into Bentley's room and he's still asleep. He looks so sweet lying in his bed and Corman is snuggled up next to him. I am overwhelmed with love and fear and peace—it's an interesting combination. I walk into the kitchen and make myself coffee. I pour myself a cup and hear tiny footsteps behind me. Bentley and Corman are standing behind me. "Good morning, buddy," I say to him with a huge smile. "How was your first night's sleep in your new bed?" He smiles and he's holding his favorite stuffed animal, a puppy. "It was good," he says. I give him a hug. It's somewhat awkward transitioning into the role of parent. But I know it will all fall into place in a matter of time.

My phone rings and it's my mom—my grandmother passed away this morning. I became a parent the same day that my grandmother died; it's a day I will never forget. Part of me thinks that my grandmother was ready to let go knowing that Bentley is safe with me—or maybe it is that I am safe with Bentley. I hang up the phone. Bentley can tell something is wrong. "What's wrong, Aunt Lolly?" he says in his sleepy voice. "Great grandmother went to heaven today, buddy," I respond. He looks sad, so I go on to explain that she lived a long, wonderful life, and it was time for her to go. I have no damn clue how to explain death to a five-year-old, so I wing it. I go with my gut instinct.

I can't believe my grandmother is gone. I don't know who to tell or what to do. I feel guilty for not being in St. Louis with my family, but I also know that I'm in a new world with Bentley—and his comfort takes priority over everything. For the first time, my needs come second to someone else's needs. It's good for me. And it's hard, but it's good. I've been thinking about myself for the past three decades out of self-preservation, and now it's time to change things up. It's time to put Bentley's needs before mine.

The first day together is stressful—I don't know what I'm doing. Corman somehow manages to cut his tail, and he's part whippet—so his tail is splattering blood all over the walls of my house. It looks like a horror movie. It's too much: my grandmother dies, I'm a new mom, and now my dog is painting the walls with his blood. My blood pressure rises. We head to grab lunch at a fast food restaurant and Bentley wants a milkshake—I'm fine with it. I want a milkshake, but I still struggle with my food and exercise obsession, so I don't order one. I'm afraid of gaining weight. I stop abruptly at a traffic light, and Bentley's milkshake spills all over the backseat, and I totally lose my cool. I get angry with him for doing that, and then after I get angry, I beat myself up for not being the perfect parent. He's a kid. He's human—it was a mistake—a mistake that I could have easily made. Why did I have to get upset with him? He starts crying and I don't know what to do. I suck at this. I am not meant to be a parent—I have enough issues of my own. What am I thinking? Seriously.

We get back home and I'm about to have a complete meltdown. I don't want Bentley to see it, so I sit him on the couch and turn the cartoons on. Corman jumps on the couch next to him to cuddle. They seem fine for the moment, so I step outside on my front steps. I sit down on the second step and I put my hands on my head. I'm staring down at the cement walkway. I bury my head between my knees because I know I'm about to completely lose it and I don't want anyone to hear me. I start sobbing. I mean—unstoppable crying. I hope Bentley can't hear me. I hope my neighbors can't hear me. My life has changed. I'm responsible for a little boy. What did I do?

THIRTEEN
Healing

Ben and I walk through the freezer section of the grocery store on a hunt for Goldfish, ice cream sandwiches, and frozen veggies for me. Well, the ice cream is for me, too. We turn into the aisle and run straight into a former colleague and his wife, both of whom I haven't seen in two or three years. By the look of surprise on their faces, they haven't heard I'd moved back to Kentucky. We exchange hellos, and then all eyes are on Bentley. "Oh," I say, fidgeting with Bentley's jacket, "this is my son, Bentley."

I still struggle with whether to introduce myself as Bentley's aunt or his mom. He has started calling me mom and that's what I am technically. Even though I can't shake the feeling that I'm intruding on my sister's turf, I have begun the process of petitioning to become Bentley's permanent guardian. I feel guilty for being his mom, like I'm diminishing my sister's role. Even though she's the reason I'm his guardian; she's the reason I'm now Ben's mom.

"Oh," they respond confused, eyebrows furrowed. "Nice to meet you, Bentley." They are at least pretending to not be so confused. I've run into other people who say, "I didn't know you had a son, Vitale." One woman said to me, "We were partying at bars five or six years ago, and you weren't pregnant then. How is this even possible?"

These moments don't discount my role in this five-year-old's life—but I'm consumed with what other people think about our arrangement. And I wonder if I'm fit to be a parent, since I can be pretty selfish. I've been doing this mom thing for nearly three months now and think I have the hang of it. During the workweek I wake Bentley up at 6:30 a.m., dress and feed him, and then drop him off at school around 7:00 a.m. It's early, but

I need to be at the office by 7:15 a.m. I pick him up from aftercare around 5:30 or 5:45 p.m. We grab takeout because I don't cook, and then we do our nighttime routine, which consists of eating dinner together, bath, books, and bed. Sometimes I feel like I'm just going through the motions; I need to be more present and engaged. I still don't have an attachment to him. I think it's partly because I'm his temporary guardian; even though I know this is a forever deal, the word "temporary" haunts me. But I know that if my sister ever gets him back, I need to trust that it's all part of God's plan. I need to focus on what's in front of me now and not worry about the future.

Bentley makes me laugh and cry and—it's like all parents say—"parenting is one of the hardest yet most rewarding jobs." I understand why it takes two people to make a baby—because it takes two people, plus a village, to raise a child. I sometimes feel resentful that I'm doing it all by myself, and then I think about my friends with kids and a husband who don't seem to have it all together either. We are all doing the best we know how to do.

My exercise and food addiction are still in full swing, but it's getting more manageable. I don't let it rule my life like I used to—and I can't because I have a child now. I try to find time for exercise between the end of the workday and when I need to get Bentley from school at 6:00 p.m. But his schedule takes priority over mine, and I don't want to model disordered eating in front of him. I'm having to unlearn all my childhood patterns and behaviors, and this will be something he will have to unlearn—and I'd rather it just be something he never learns—and then he never has to unlearn it.

Like any five-year-old, Bentley can pick up on my nonverbal communication and my facial expressions and my body language. I need to be careful about what I say and do in front of him. I don't want him to take on my bullshit. I can already tell that he thinks it's his responsibility to make me happy. If I'm anxious or worried or stressed, he says, "I love you, Mom," over and over. He does that because he thinks it will make me happy. That's a behavior I know he adopted to help my mother feel better, just like I did when I was a kid. And now he's saying it because he thinks it will work on me. "Bentley, I love you, too," I respond. I pull him close to me and put his hands in mine. I look him straight in the eyes. "I want you to know that it's not your job to make me happy. It's my job to make me happy. I love when you tell me you love me, but don't say it just to make me happy. Okay?" I'm having a grown-up conversation with a child. At least all the years of therapy and the work I've been doing in sobriety are paying off. "Okay, Mom," he says back to me.

I'm still single—it has been about six months now—and it's fine. I don't have any time to think about it because I've been learning the ropes of single parenting. The one major lesson I'm learning in all this parenting stuff is that I can't do it all myself. Which I hate admitting, but I start accepting help when I need it.

One of the moms at Ben's school has taken me under her wing, and I'm grateful. She invites us over for playdates and sleepovers and even offers to take Bentley to his soccer practice each week, and I allow myself to accept the help. It's not easy, but I understand God wants me to learn how to receive and accept help. I am learning to love the lessons he puts in my life.

My phone is ringing, and it says "mom" on the caller ID. My heart sinks. What does she want now? She's been drinking a lot recently; I can tell on our phone conversations. Not playing the role of Bentley's parent has affected her deeply. And she's using alcohol and Xanax to try to cope with it. And although I understand why she's doing what she's doing, it's too much for me to deal with. It's too damn much. Every time I answer her phone calls, I expect it to be drunk mom because that's what I usually get. I don't want to answer the call; I want to pretend that she's sober and that I don't have to deal with this. "This" is exactly why I became Bentley's guardian.

"Hey, Mom," I say. "What's up?" She hates when I say "what's up" because she thinks I'm attacking her, but it's just my normal phone greeting. I need to work on not saying that when she calls, but I always forget. Why do I need to change for her anyway?

"Hello, Vitale," she says. My heart sinks—she *is* drunk. "I was just wanting to call and see how you're doing."

Yeah, right. She must need something. I always let my guard down with her. I don't want to, but I do. I always expect her to be something she's not capable of being—my mom. She's not capable of loving me the way I want her to love me. And it breaks my heart, over and over again. We get into some argument over Bentley and my parenting style. She wants to be in control since she no longer has control. "You're a terrible mom, and all you do is think about yourself," she screams. I can't take it. She can't just call me and tell me shit like that. She doesn't know anything about how I parent—and for fuck's sake—I'm doing the best I know how to do. I scream back at her and she hangs up on me—which is a classic Mom move. I put the phone down and tears stream down my face. I just want to be loved and understood. I just want my mom to be my mom. My heart is broken once again.

I'm a little more than two years sober, and I continue to work my program—I need it especially right now. I go to two AA meetings a week; I meet with my sponsor weekly and I belong to a women's Step study group that meets on Sundays. I'm showing up and I'm doing the work.

* * *

Even though I have a love-hate relationship with my mother, I still want her in my life—even if she hurts me. She's coming to visit Bentley and me this weekend. I haven't forgotten the fact that she called me a bad mom, but I still yearn for her love. She's on her way to Lexington and I can't get a hold of her. She normally calls me when she gets on the road, but not today. And that makes me nervous. Normally when she doesn't answer her phone, it's because she's been drinking or taking pills. I try calling my dad to figure out what's going on and he's not answering either. I pace around the house, stressed out.

A few hours later, I finally get her on the phone, and I can tell she's messed up. I don't know if it's alcohol or pills, but it's one of the two. What the fuck am I going to do with her when she gets here? I can't handle being around her when she's drunk. I call my sponsor and we come up with a game plan: let her arrive and stay the night and when she sobers up the next day ask her to leave. I need to set boundaries and expectations. And Bentley doesn't need to be around this.

My mom finally arrives. She gets out of the car and I am right—she's messed up. I can't control my anger. I always plan to control my anger, but whenever it comes down to practicing kindness in the moment, I'm unable to. There's too much history between us—too much pain. It's 3:00 p.m., and thankfully Bentley has church camp tonight, so he won't be home until 7:30 p.m. and he goes to bed immediately. At least my mom has time to sober up, and if she doesn't sober up, then Ben will only have a little exposure to her intoxication. Why did I allow her into my house again?

My mom is still intoxicated when Bentley comes home, so I do my best to shield Bentley from her. At least I'm here with him. At least I'm providing him with a sober, healthy home. A consistent home and routine. I give him a shower and put him to bed. I let my mom participate but only on the periphery. He's finally asleep and my mom is outside on my back porch smoking. I pray for the right words to say to her. I ask God to speak through me with love because God knows I struggle with that. She finally comes into the house.

"Mom, we need to talk," I tell her.

"Um, okay," she responds. She flops herself on my couch and I sit in the flowery upholstered chair that's across from her.

"Mom, this is unacceptable," I say. "You can't keep doing this. You aren't allowed back at my house unless you're sober." There's an awkward pause.

"Whatever, Vitale. You're always calling the shots. Whatever you want, you get," she says mockingly.

"How am I supposed to love you like this?" I ask. I genuinely want to know. "How do I love you when you don't want to get help? How do I have a relationship with you like this when it's not healthy for me?" We go back and forth with no resolution. I let her sleep in my bed. I put a pillow and blanket out for me on the couch.

I can't sleep. My mind is racing, and my body is coursing with anger and resentment. I close my eyes and repeat the serenity prayer over and over in my head, "God, grant me the serenity to accept the things I cannot change, the courage to change the things I can, and the wisdom to know the difference."

I wake up the next day and my mom rides with me to drop off Bentley at school. There's no conversation between us—the only words spoken are directed toward Bentley. He gets out of the car and says goodbye. "Have a great day, bub. I love you," I say. He thinks he's going to see his grandmother after school, but she's not allowed to stay. Not after last night. We get home and go out to the back porch. My mom lights up a cigarette. She's sober this morning and I can tell she's somewhat remorseful about her behavior. She won't look me in the eyes; she just stares at the ground. She is always agreeable and sweet and kind after a night of drinking and bad behavior. She doesn't want to talk about it because she never does. But that's not how I live my life now. I deal with things. I sit across from her and I look her in the eyes. I start crying. "Mom, I don't want to do this," I say. "But you're going to need to leave. You're not allowed to stay here after your behavior last night." She doesn't want to leave, and she gets somewhat angry with me. But she packs her bags and leaves. I'm standing behind my screen door, crying as I watch her car drive down my street. I just want my mom. I just want her to love me.

* * *

My aunt Catheryn and I have grown close during this time. As a new mom, I need parenting advice and I'm sure not getting any help from my mom. So I seek help from my aunt. She has a background in early child development, plus both of my cousins are well adjusted, so she must have done something right. It feels good to have someone in my corner, someone who tells me I'm doing a good job and someone who can give me advice on how to handle certain situations. She's completely shocked by my mom's recent behavior and she validates what a big deal it is. She understands the gravity of it all.

There's chaos in Alabama. It seems that my mom has gone off the deep end again with her drinking and Xanax. I know she's hurting, but it doesn't lessen my pain. She doesn't call a lot, which is always a sign that she's not doing well. And my dad is still enabling; he doesn't want to deal with or admit that she has a problem, and when he does admit it, he minimizes the severity of it.

I drop Bentley off at school and I take my usual route to work. It's still dark outside and there aren't many cars on the road at 7:15 a.m., and I like it that way. My phone rings, and it's my dad. Hmm. I wonder what he's calling about. "Vitale," he says seriously. "Your mom has decided to go to rehab. She's going to the same place that you went. I'm going to take her in the next day or two." I'm speechless. I have hoped and prayed for this moment. Rehab completely changed my life and maybe it can change hers, too. I start crying happy tears.

My mom being in rehab opens the door to internal reflection. I didn't realize how much time and energy I spent worrying about her. And now she's somewhere safe, and I don't have to worry about her. And now I have time to focus on me. And it's scary. I have a lot of demons that I need to deal with. And I have nothing but Bentley to distract me. I have no man in my life, my mom is in rehab, and I'm working through my disordered eating. I have lots of time for introspection.

The last time I pondered codependency was when I was in rehab. But now, with the space I have to explore it, I see how my codependency is off the charts. I've been allowing my mom's feelings to dictate my feelings all my life. If she's sober, I'm happy. If she's not sober, I'm not happy. I realize that I've been calling and checking on her nearly every day, and I used that as a thermostat for my mood. Now it's time for me to take charge of my feelings—not anyone else's.

My mom's been in rehab for a few weeks and I start living my life differently. I've been focusing on myself for the first time. This is the first time in sobriety that I'm finally understanding my family dynamic and my own dysfunction and coping mechanisms. I'm connecting the dots with my need for control and perfection and how that translates into my exercise schedule and eating habits. I'm finally understanding my pattern of toxic relationships, with Tom and Jack in particular; that my own feelings of unworthiness attract people with their own feelings of unworthiness. I understand now that my outside world is just a reflection of my inside world. These revelations are a byproduct of my mom being in rehab; they are a byproduct of me releasing my codependency.

My energy and my self-worth are shifting. I feel like the first two years of sobriety were spent just trying to figure out my new normal: learning how to dance at weddings sober, learning what to do with my hands at parties when I no longer had a glass in them, learning how to feel my feelings, transferring one addiction to another, feeling lonely and knowing it's temporary—knowing that everything in life, the good and the bad, is temporary. I have been learning to put one foot in front of the other without drugs and alcohol. I am going to meetings and doing step work and reaching out to people in the sober community. I am doing as I am told. And now I'm almost two-and-a-half years sober and I've graduated from early sobriety. Now I'm ready to do the real work. The hard work.

FOURTEEN
The Next Chapter

I think I'm ready to date again, but I don't know where to start. I don't party anymore, and I don't go to bars. A first date sounds terrifying. When do I tell him that I'm in recovery? Do I tell him immediately, or wait until after a few dates? And what about having sex sober? Now that I think about it, I haven't had much sober sex. And then there's the fact that I have a child—how will I deal with that? I've never really "dated." I either met guys at bars and went home with them, or I got locked into a serious relationship immediately. And I don't think I want to date anyone who is in recovery; it would be too much AA program for me. I've been so caught up in my exercise and food obsession, that dating hasn't even been a thought for me. The fact that I'm considering it shows growth. It shows healing. And I'm lonely. I want to date someone new, not someone from my past. I want a fresh start; I want to create a new kind of partnership, one that reflects my new lifestyle and values. Dating in recovery and dating with a child are scary and not very sexy. "Hi, I'm sober and I have a kid." But I guess I don't need to have all of that figured out right now. Just being open to dating is a start.

And I feel my heart opening to a lot of other new things—being a mom full-time, exploring my past without shame or judgment, establishing boundaries with my parents and sister, attracting a partner who loves me for me, healing my traumas and insecurities, and most importantly—finding love and acceptance for myself. My heart is opening, and I am changing.

* * *

The relationship with my mom and dad grows tense. It's the holidays and they want me home. We are in a major disagreement—my mom has relapsed since her time in rehab and she's drinking regularly again. And I don't want to be around it. I don't want Bentley to be around it. I need something to help me cope with my family's dysfunction. I need to learn how to stop being codependent. I need to learn how not to be controlled by my parents. I need to learn how to become my own person, whatever that means.

I heard about a new group that has formed a chapter near me recently—Adult Children of Alcoholics (ACA). And it sounds like a good fit. I'm an adult and I'm the child of an alcoholic. I start attending the meetings in January 2017. The topics are intense, and the work is deep soul work. I know it's the right place for me, but there's part of me that's scared to look at my childhood and past trauma. There's part of me that wants to resist it. Subconsciously I know this is going to be painful, yet profound, work. And something in my life needs to change. I've outgrown AA, and ACA feels like home to me. With AA I feel like I've hit a ceiling. I am interested in the reasons I might be an addict in the first place, and ACA helps me explore that. It validates the trauma and repercussions of a child exposed to alcoholism her entire life. There are other people in the room who know what it's like to grow up in an alcoholic home. None of my friends understand what it's like, so it's powerful to be surrounded by people who get it. It's a Twelve-step program, just like AA, except I describe this program as learning about self-love and re-parenting yourself. It's about becoming your own loving parent. It sounds hokey, but it touches something I crave; mothering and nurturing, a feeling of being safe. My parents are driving me crazy—especially now that I'm raising their grandson, and I need to figure out how to deal and cope with it in a healthy way.

I start regularly attending one to two ACA meetings a week. The work is powerful. I've cried in several of the meetings, and some of my childhood memories are coming back to me—memories that I buried deep. This work is leading to a level of self-actualization that I've never experienced before. In AA, it's all about taking responsibility for your actions, and I've never had a problem with that before. I have a problem with taking too much responsibility. I always want to fix and manipulate people to make myself feel needed. ACA is all about seeing our parents' role in our life and knowing that we aren't responsible for the trauma in our childhood. We are responsible for the healing of it, but it's not our fault the trauma happened.

I'm doing this deep work and it's uncovering shit I don't want to deal with because this work requires me bringing up my body shame and being molested by my daycare provider when I was three. It's bringing up the generational pain and trauma that my parents passed down to me—the feelings of shame, unworthiness, guilt, and perfection. It's uncovering memories of being so alone and abandoned as a child; the success disparities between me and my sister; the body shame I've carried with me my whole life; my pattern of numbing with outside substances. So many memories and feelings and emotions that I buried for decades. They are all coming to the surface. And at the same time, I feel suffocated when parenting Bentley. And when I feel suffocated or trapped, I shut down. I need my freedom. It's like I'm in a padded room and I'm beating on the walls to get out, but no one will let me out. I do find it interesting that my feelings are coinciding with my ninth month as Bentley's full-time mom. I bet this is what all moms experience during pregnancy, except I wasn't pregnant so I'm experiencing it now. The fact that I'm a mom has set in. The reality of it all is hitting me. I'm a parent. Holy fuck. I'm not babysitting. I'm parenting, forever.

My parents want to spend time with Bentley, which I'm indifferent about, but I don't want to cause more tension. And more important, I do care that Bentley needs to see his grandparents. Even though they are unhealthy, he has a special relationship with them, and I don't want to take that away from him or my parents. We go to Huntsville for a long weekend. I'm uneasy about Bentley being around my mom because of her unpredictable behavior, but at least I will be there the entire time in case anything happens. I just need to get this done so I can cross it off the list. Bentley has spent time with his grandparents. Check.

* * *

I've been Bentley's temporary guardian for a year, and I need the title change for my own well-being. I've been involved in the process for months now, and I'm ready for it to feel more permanent. My heart has been closed off to him, unintentionally. I've been afraid to love him all out, afraid that my sister could yank him away from me. It's our court day today. My parents are happy to transfer their permanent guardianship to me; my mom has had a year to accept it. We have to go through the judge, and we all need to be interviewed by Bentley's attorney ad litem. I am asked to prepare a photo album of our year together to show my fitness as a parent. I take pictures of my home, but I make sure the house isn't too clean, so it doesn't seem staged.

My parents are interviewed and then Bentley is interviewed separately. I tell him to be honest and to be himself, not to be scared. I'm the last interview conducted by Bentley's guardian ad litem, and I'm nervous. I'm a recovering drug addict and I'm single; what if that's a problem? I know that everything is in God's hands, but I'm still scared. I'm about to be interviewed by a complete stranger and he is going to evaluate me and judge me as a parent based on some pictures and a thirty-minute interview.

I sit down in the chair and my body is tense. My hands are in my lap and my ankles are crossed. I want to seem professional. There are so many questions, but it's the last few that get me. "So, you're a recovering drug addict. Tell me about that. What do you do for your recovery? Do you have a sponsor? Do you take any prescription drugs? So you take an antidepressant. Tell me about your depression. Is it a problem? Have you ever thought about committing suicide?" Question after question, after question. I feel like my entire history is being dissected and judged. I am not prepared for all these questions. I am not prepared for the emotional fallout I am experiencing. Before the interview is over, there is one final question. "Does your sister know that you are seeking permanent custody?" he asks. I can't lie; I want to become Bentley's permanent guardian fair and square. I don't want to manipulate anything. "She doesn't know about this," I answer honestly. Frankie knows I was granted temporary guardianship a year ago, but she has no idea I am pursuing permanent guardianship. It would make it too real for her. With temporary guardianship, she could pretend I was babysitting. There is no pretending anymore.

"Well, I'm going to need to contact her. Legally she needs to be notified so she can have the opportunity to contest the transfer of guardianship." That hadn't even occurred to me. The interview is finished, and I go back to the main reception area. It's out of my control.

Our lawyer comes back to tell us that the attorney ad litem contacted my sister and she is on her way. She then proceeds to tell us that Bentley's attorney is also recommending that I become Bentley's permanent guardian—that it is in Bentley's best interest. That feels good.

It's time for the court hearing to begin. I usher in and sit at the table on the left. The courtroom is cold and barren. Our lawyer instructs me and my mom to not say anything—no matter what—that she would handle all the comments. And she also reminds us that the judge is the same judge that awarded my parents custody of Bentley a few years ago, so she's on our side. We are almost through the hearing when my sister and her latest boyfriend burst through the courtroom doors.

"Judge, I didn't know anything about this hearing. I want to contest it," my sister screams. "I don't agree with Vitale getting permanent custody." The judge gives my sister a look of disdain and then warns her she will be in contempt of court if she speaks out of turn again. "You need to sit down," says the judge. "And you may only speak when I address you."

"Yes ma'am," my sister says sheepishly. My heart races. I can't believe this is happening. It's like an episode of *Judge Judy*. The judge asks my sister to stand up. "I see that you are pregnant," she says.

"Yes ma'am, I am," my sister responds.

"If I made you take a drug test right now, would you pass?" the judge asks.

"Well, I've been smoking pot, but I was in Colorado," my sister says.

Jesus. If she's willing to admit to pot, who knows what else is in her system.

"Well, the decision has already been made," informs the judge. "I'm awarding permanent custody to Vitale Buford. Court adjourned."

The gavel drops. I stand numb. I can't look at my sister. It's June 27, 2017, and I am now the permanent guardian of Bentley.

* * *

It feels good—me and Bentley . . . it's a God thing. It wouldn't have happened if it wasn't meant to. I finally have permission to love Bentley with my whole heart. I'm not afraid of Bentley being taken away from me because that's not the point. The point is what's best for him, not me. I get to be his mom for the rest of his life.

People always say, "Bentley is so lucky to have you." But I know the truth—I'm the lucky one. Bentley is teaching me how to live my life and to love unconditionally. He's helping me heal everything: my addictions, my disordered eating, my pain, my relentless search for love. He's healing my perfectionism. I'm ready for the next phase of my life. I'm ready to continue the healing process. I am ready for the journey ahead of me.

Postscript

This book was a labor of love and courage. It forced me to confront parts of my story that I had hidden for so long—and although it was painful at times, I am forever grateful for the opportunity. Writing my story is one of the scariest things I've ever done. And if you know me—I always do the scary thing. And that included me owning my story, even the parts of it that really hurt. For as much bad as I shared in my book, there is also so much good. My relationship with my parents has grown and evolved—and although there have been really difficult times—the one thing that is constant is their love for me. They have always supported my dreams, no matter how big or crazy. They have always encouraged me to follow my heart. And for that I am forever grateful. Mom and Dad—thank you for giving me the courage to get sober. Thank you for giving me the courage to follow my dreams.

Acknowledgments

My story has been in the works my entire life, but it wasn't until I got sober that I was inspired to truly own my story and allow it to unfold. I am deeply grateful to the following people for loving me, inspiring me and believing in me:

Bentley—you are my heart and my mirror and my love. Your sweet little soul brings out the best in me.

Mom and Dad—thank you for supporting my dreams. I wouldn't be here without you.

Lynn—you listened to all the pieces of my story and were my endless source of encouragement. You have been a huge part of my healing journey and I don't know where I would be without your friendship.

Stan—you are my forever lovemate. You see me as I truly am. I didn't know a love like ours was possible. Thank you for supporting me in this process and believing in my dreams.

My girlfriends—thank you for loving me through it all. You all are my family. Meredith—thank you for being there for *all* of it and still loving me; Anne—thank you for always holding up the mirror for me; Moochie—thank you for rescuing me during one of my darkest times; Manda—thank you for seeing me as I am; Rush—thank you for your kindness and for really getting me. My friend family is incredible, and I wouldn't be here without you. Esther, Tru Blu, Mary Quinn—thank you.

Aunt Steph—thank you for encouraging me and for always listening and understanding.

Justin—thank you for opening my eyes: *I see in you what I refuse to see in me.*

Nicole—thank you for understanding the darkness and for helping me let my light shine.

DeVere—thank you for being the one who truly understands.

All of the people who believed in my story and made it come to life—Francesca and Changing Lives Press; Michele—thank you a million times over for truly seeing and understanding my story; Cathy—thank you for coaching me; and Dr. Mangine—thank you for your kind counsel and guidance.

There are so many other people who love and support me—thank you to each of you. Xoxo

#yolo #letsdothis